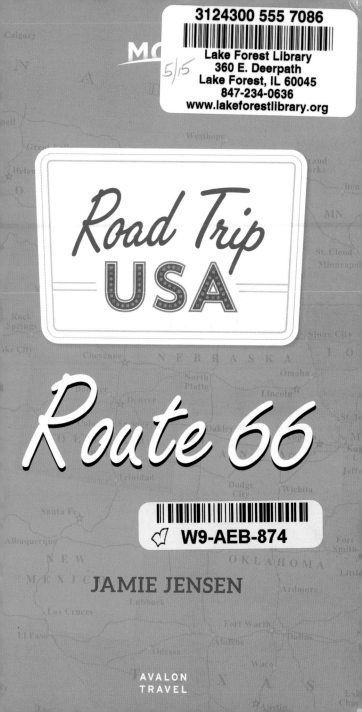

MC

Road Trip USA

Route 66

W9-AEB-874

JAMIE JENSEN

AVALON
TRAVEL

CONTENTS

New Mexico Art Museum, Santa Fe, New Mexico

Route
66

The Grand Canyon — pg. 86

◄ 420 mi ►   pg. 98   pg. 113   400 mi ►   pg. 62

Hollywood Forever

London Bridge

Tinkertown

If you're looking for great displays of neon signs, mom-and-pop motels in the middle of nowhere, or kitschy Americana, do as the song says and "get your kicks on Route 66."

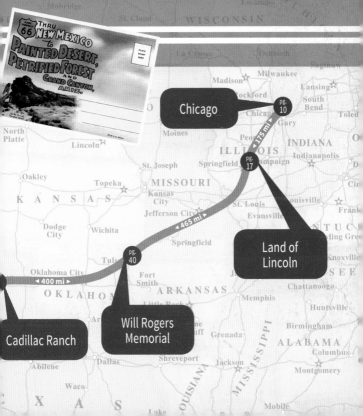

Between Chicago, Illinois, and Los Angeles, California

The romance of Route 66 continues to captivate people around the world. Running between Chicago and Los Angeles, "over two thousand miles all the way" in the words of the popular R&B anthem, this legendary old road passes through the heart of the United States on a diagonal trip that takes in some of the country's most archetypal roadside scenes. If you're looking for great displays of neon signs, rusty middle-of-nowhere truck stops, or kitschy Americana, do as the song says and "get your kicks on Route 66."

But perhaps the most compelling reason to follow Route 66 is to experience the road's ingrained time line of contemporary America. Before it was called Route 66, and long before it was even paved in 1926, this corridor was traversed by the National Old Trails Highway, one of the country's first transcontinental highways. For three decades before and after World War II, Route 66 earned the title **"Main Street of America"** because it wound through small towns across the Midwest and Southwest, lined by hundreds of cafés, motels, gas stations, and tourist attractions. During the Great Depression, hundreds of thousands of farm families, displaced from the Dust Bowl, made their way west along Route 66 to California, following what John Steinbeck called **"The Mother Road"** in his vivid portrait, *The Grapes of Wrath.* After World War II, many thousands more expressed their upward mobility by leaving the industrial East, bound for good jobs in the suburban idyll of Southern California—again following Route 66, which came to embody the demographic shift from the Rust Belt to the Sun Belt.

Beginning in the late 1950s and continuing gradually over the next 25 years, old Route 66 was bypassed section by section as the high-speed Interstate highways were completed. Finally, after the last stretch of freeway was completed in 1984, Route 66 was officially decommissioned. The old route is now designated Historic Route 66.

Though it is no longer a main route across the country, Route 66 has retained its mystique in

part due to the very same effective hype, hucksterism, and boosterism that animated it through its half-century heyday. It was a Route 66 sight, the marvelous **Meramec Caverns**, that gave the world the bumper sticker. And it was here on Route 66 that the great American driving vacation first flourished. Billboards and giant statues along the highway still hawk a baffling array of roadside attractions, tempting passing travelers to view giant blue whales, to see live rattlesnakes and other wild creatures on display in roadside menageries, or to stay at "Tucumcari Tonite."

The same commercial know-how and shameless self-promotion has helped the towns along the old route stay alive. Diners and motels play up their Route 66 connections, and many bona fide Route 66 landmarks are kept in business by nostalgic travelers intent on experiencing a taste of this endlessly endangered American experience. That said, many quirky old motels and cafés hang on by a thread of hope, sit vacant, or survive in memory only—all for want of an Interstate exit. In fact, of all the roads covered in this book, Route 66 has perhaps felt the greatest impact from the modern Interstate world; for many stretches you'll be forced to leave the old two-lane and follow the super slabs that have been built right on top of the old road.

Route 66 passes through a marvelous cross-section of American scenes, from the cornfields of Illinois all the way to the golden sands and sunshine of Los Angeles, passing by such diverse environs as the **Grand Canyon**, the Native American communities of the desert Southwest, the small-town Midwest heartlands of **Oklahoma** and **the Ozarks**, as well as the gritty streets of **St. Louis** and **Chicago**. Whether you are motivated by an interest in history, feel a nostalgic yearning for the "good old days" Route 66 has come to represent, or simply want to experience firsthand the amazing diversity of people and landscapes that line its path, Route 66 offers an unforgettable journey into America, then and now.

ILLINOIS

Heading diagonally across the state between Chicago and St. Louis, what remains of Route 66 is a surprisingly rural cruise through endless fields of corn. Despite the urban conglomerations at both ends, for most of its nearly 300-mile trek here, Route 66 and its modern usurper, I-55, pass along flat prairies with nary a smokestack or skyscraper as far as the eye can see.

The heavy industrial and poverty-stricken hinterlands of Chicago and East St. Louis aren't terribly rewarding for travelers in search of the Mother Road, but a couple of intriguing attractions—one a prehistoric city, the other a water tower shaped like a catsup bottle—are worth searching out. The only real city along Route 66 is the Illinois state capital, **Springfield,** which has preserved its sections of Route 66 alongside a wealth of places connected to the namesake president here in the "Land of Lincoln." Dozens of small towns across the state play up their Route 66 connections, and most boast at least one true old-road landmark.

Route 66 Across Chicagoland

Following the first (or last) leg of Route 66 across Chicago and its hinterlands is really not worth the effort for anyone except the most die-hard end-to-ender—even Jack Rittenhouse, in his original 1946 *A Guide Book to Highway 66,* didn't bother to describe the route until it reached Plainfield, 35 miles southwest of the Loop, and these days the Chicagoland suburbs don't fade away until you get beyond Joliet.

A little piece of highway history happened in 1926 when the original alignment of Route 66 crossed the even older Lincoln Highway, America's first transcontinental road, later marked on maps as US-30. The Lincoln Highway and Route 66 intersected first at Joliet and later further west at Plainfield.

For a symbolic starting point, you can use the grand old Art Institute of Chicago in Grant Park along the lakeshore, since the last US-66 shield used to hang from a streetlight just south of the gallery. If Chicago is your "end of the road," you'll probably prefer to avoid the final few

miles of surface streets and make your way to town as quickly as possible via I-55, celebrating your arrival with a cup of coffee at Lou Mitchell's.

From Lake Michigan, the old road ran westbound through the Loop via Adams Street (take Jackson Boulevard eastbound; both are one-way) before angling southwest along Ogden Avenue—a long, diagonal exception to the city's main grid of streets.

Ogden Avenue, which carries Route 66 in and out of Chicago, is not one of the world's scenic wonders, but it can reveal a lot about the places it passes through. Located just south of Frank Lloyd Wright's hometown of Oak Park, **Cicero** is notorious for its connections to another local legend: mobster Al Capone, who took refuge here outside the jurisdiction of the Chicago police. Cicero's main Route 66 connection is the fine sign marking **Henry's Drive-In** (6031 W. Ogden Ave., 708/656-9344), where you can snack on excellent Polish hot dogs smothered with a pile of french fries.

Bounded by the I-55 freeway, **Berwyn** effectively marks one end of this first or last stretch of Route 66 with the unusual **Chicago Portage National Historic Site.** This 100-acre semi-wilderness, surrounded by decrepit and aban-

Chicago

New York may have bigger and better museums, shops, and restaurants, and even Los Angeles has more people, but Chicago is still the most all-American city, and one of the most exciting and enjoyable places to visit in the world. After shrinking for decades as its suburbs grew and grew, Chicago seems to have stabilized. The city reinvents and re-invests in itself, with new parks, art galleries, and condo towers, as a new generation discovers the plea-

modern-day Michigan Avenue Bridge

sures of urban life. Commerce capital of Middle America, Chicago's location at the crossroads between the settled East and the wide-open West has helped it to give birth to many new things we now take for granted: the skyscraper, the blues, and the atomic bomb (not to mention Oprah and Obama!).

Away from the Loop, the skyscraper-spiked lakefront business district that holds North America's tallest and most impressive collection of modern architecture in its oblong square mile, much of Chicago is surprisingly low-rise and residential. Also surprising, considering its inland location, is that Chicago has a high percentage of immigrants—200,000 Poles form one of the largest communities outside Poland, and Hispanics constitute nearly 29 percent of Chicago's population of close to three million—with a multi-ethnic character readily apparent in numerous enclaves all over the city. Whatever their origin, however, residents take a particular pride in identifying themselves as Chicagoans, and despite the city's rusting infrastructure, their good-natured enthusiasm for the place can be contagious.

For an unbeatable introduction to Chicago, hop aboard a river cruise offered by the **Chicago Architecture Foundation** (312/922-8697, daily Apr.-Nov. only, $38). Departing from where the Michigan Avenue Bridge crosses the river and Wacker Drive, these informative and enjoyable tours offer an unusual look up at the city's magnificent towers. Enthusiastic expert guides give the city's general historical background as well as pointed architectural history. North from the river, the

"Magnificent Mile" of Michigan Avenue is a bustling shopping strip that holds yet more distinctive towers, along with many of the city's top shops, restaurants, and hotels. Starting with the gothic-style Tribune Tower—decorated with bits of famous buildings and monuments stolen by Tribune staffers from around the globe—and running past the circa-1869 Historic Water Tower at its midpoint, the "Mag Mile" ends in the north with the 95-story John Hancock Center.

Along the lakefront at the heart of downtown, the **Art Institute of Chicago** (111 S. Michigan Ave., 312/443-3600, $23) boasts one of the world's great collections of 19th- and 20th-century French painting and a broad survey of fine art from all over the world. Among its many fine paintings, the institute gives pride of place to Grant Wood's *American Gothic,* which he painted as a student and sold to the institute for $300. North and east of the museum's beautiful Modern Wing is Chicago's latest great claim to fame: **Millennium Park,** a 25-acre public garden full of fabulous sculptures and a magical, Frank Gehry-designed outdoor concert pavilion that's home to numerous summer concerts and events.

More than just another baseball game, watching the **Chicago Cubs** play at **Wrigley Field** (1060 Addison St., 773/404-2827) is a rite of passage that taps into the deepest meanings of the national pastime. Ivy covers the redbrick outfield walls and Chicagoans of all stripes root on the perennial not-quite-winners. The "other" Chicago baseball team, the **White Sox,** play at modern **U.S. Cellular Field** (333 W. 35th St., 312/674-1000), south of the Loop alongside I-94.

PRACTICALITIES

Chicago is home to one of America's busiest and most infuriating airports, O'Hare (ORD), 17 miles northwest of the Loop and well served by Chicago Transit Authority (CTA) subway trains, shuttle services, and taxis. Chicago's other airport, Midway, is closer to the center of town, and Chicago is also the hub of the national Amtrak system, with trains pulling in to Union Station from all over the country. To get around, you'll really be better off leaving the car behind and riding the CTA elevated train—better known as the "L"—which serves the entire city almost around the clock.

Chicago has all sorts of top-quality, cutting-edge-cuisine restaurants, but to get a feel for the city you'll be better off stopping at the many

(continued on next page)

(continued)

older places that have catered to Chicagoans forever. Near the start of old Route 66, **Lou Mitchell's** (565 W. Jackson Blvd., 312/939-3111) is one of the greatest breakfast and lunch places on the planet. Along with deep-dish pizza (as served at Uno's, Pizzeria Due, etc.), hot dogs a.k.a. red hots a.k.a. Polish sausages are a real Chicago specialty that can be sampled at a dozen world-class spots. Try them at **Jim's Original** (1250 S. Union Ave, 312/733-7820, open 24 hours daily), just west of the I-90 Dan Ryan Expressway. Farther from downtown, toward O'Hare, there's **Superdawg Drive-In** (6363 N. Milwaukee Ave., 773/763-0660), where you can soak up the 1940s character.

Places to stay in Chicago include the moderate likes of the **Best Western River North** (125 W. Ohio St., 312/467-0800, $142 and up), in the trendy River North gallery district, which offers free parking within a quick walk of the Magnificent Mile along Michigan Avenue. Chicago's classiest older hotel is the **Drake Hotel** (140 E. Walton Pl., 312/787-2200, $195 and up), just off the lake, with elegant public areas and gracious staff. Even if you only soak up the exuberant 1920s Moorish-style lobby, or go for a swim in the palatial 14th-floor pool, the most fabulous place to stay could be the **InterContinental** (505 N. Michigan Ave., 312/944-4100, $180 and up), though the smallish rooms expose the truth that the building started life as a Shriner's health club.

The best source of detailed information is the **Chicago Office of Tourism** (877/244-2246).

Superdawg Drive-In

doned industrial lands, preserves the place where early explorers learned to carry their canoes and boats between the Chicago and Des Plaines watersheds, linking the Atlantic Ocean and Gulf of Mexico via the Great Lakes and Mississippi River. (Today, the euphemistically named Chicago Sanitary and Ship Canal serves a similar role, running via Lockport and Joliet.)

One longstanding Route 66 landmark stands about 20 miles outside Chicago in Willowbrook, off Hwy-83 on the north side of I-55: **Dell Rhea's Chicken Basket** (645 Joliet Rd., 630/325-0780) is a welcoming old roadside tavern, with famously fabulous chicken dinners and frequent live music.

Joliet

Joliet, the "City of Steel and Stone," has a rough reputation that doesn't really reflect its status as the fastest growing city in Illinois. Route 66 through this once-mighty industrial enclave is a feast for fans of post-industrial scenery. Loads of old warehouses and commercial buildings like the lovely Rialto Theater on Chicago Street line the route. Stalwart bridges cross the Des Plaines River and historic Illinois & Michigan Canal, which, beginning in the 1840s, connected Chicago with the Mississippi River before being replaced by the less salubrious Sanitary and Ship Canal.

While the suburbs grow and grow, efforts to reverse downtown's long economic downturn by embracing casino gambling have not had much success. The large **Harrah's Joliet Casino** (151 N. Joliet St., 815/740-7800) draws gamblers but has not done much to revive the waterfront or the surrounding streets.

South of Joliet, following old Route 66 (Hwy-53) across the I-80 superslab brings you past the massive **Chicagoland Speedway** and the **Route 66 Raceway** (888/629-7223), where NHRA drag races, NASCAR stock car races, and occasional pop music concerts are held. Also in Joliet, along the Des Plaines River north of downtown, is the now-closed state prison from which John Belushi (a.k.a. "Joliet Jake") is released at the beginning of the 1980 movie *The Blues Brothers.*

Midewin National Tallgrass Prairie Preserve

Along Route 66 between Joliet and Wilmington, a unique partnership between environmentalists and the U.S. military is working to re-create the natural ecosystem on one of the most environmentally damaged areas imaginable: 19,000 acres of the old Joliet ammunition factory are being converted into the **Midewin National Tallgrass**

Prairie Preserve (815/423-6370, trails open daily, welcome center open Mon.-Sat. in summer, Mon.-Fri. in winter). Since 1996, when the land was transferred from the U.S. Army to the U.S. Forest Service, the change from producing TNT to regrowing the native tallgrass prairie has been slow and steady. After years of toxic clean-ups and careful husbandry, more than half the old plant has been returned to its natural state and now offers more than 20 miles of hiking and biking trails on both sides of Hwy-53 (old Route 66). Midewin (pronounced "mi-DAY-win") is a native Potawatomi word meaning "healthy balance," and a visit here gives a good feeling for the flora and fauna that would have existed naturally in places like this all over the Midwest.

Hwy-53: Wilmington and Dwight

From Joliet, you can follow old Route 66 southwest through a series of nice small towns along Hwy-53, which runs along the southeast side of I-55. Though the route is sometimes a bit obscure and not all that rich in history or aesthetic delights, the towns here offer a very pleasant taste of what old Route 66 had to offer.

Wilmington is semi-famous for its photogenic 30-foot-tall, bright green **Gemini Giant** statue, which stands in front of the former Launching Pad Drive-In (810 E. Baltimore St.). The Gemini Giant is in fine shape, but not its host; the Launching Pad has been closed and put up for sale for a number of years. Fortunately, for hungry road-trippers, the neighboring town of **Braidwood** has the popular, retro-1950s **Polk-A-Dot Drive-In** (222 N. Front St., 815/458-3377) along old Route 66.

Continuing along Hwy-53, there are a couple more classic Route 66 scenes along the old road northwest of Pontiac, the next biggish town. **Dwight** is leafy and quaint, well known a century ago for its Keeley Institute treatment center for alcoholics, and now famous for its fine old Texaco station, which stands at the main crossroads (near the reliable Old Route 66 Family Restaurant). The Dwight Texaco station opened in 1933 and managed to stay in business until 1999, earning it a reputation as the oldest surviving gas station on the Mother Road (retiring at the ripe old age of 66 was a clever marketing move!). The station has been restored to its original look and now serves as Dwight's welcome center. To my eye, an even more picturesque old Standard Oil gas station stands just down Hwy-53 in the next Route 66 town, **Odell.**

Pontiac: Route 66 Hall of Fame

Some 90 miles southeast of Lake Michigan, the former coal-mining town of **Pontiac** (pop. 11,931) surrounds the stately, circa-1875 Livingston County Courthouse. The courthouse's green lawns hold the usual battery of monuments, including one to the namesake Ottawa chief whose visage also graced the General Motors marquee. According to the WPA *Guide to Illinois*, another of these monuments, the Soldiers and Sailors Monument, received the shortest presidential dedication in history when,

A short stretch of original, circa 1926-era Route 66 near **Lexington,** right off the south side of I-55 exit 178, has been decorated with replicas of old billboards and Burma-Shave advertisements, and dubbed **Memory Lane.** It's officially a pedestrian and bike-only section of Morris Street.

in 1902, it was "dedicated with a few hasty words by President Theodore Roosevelt, before an audience of less than a dozen people, who congregated briefly under a terrific downpour."

Though the old road ran around rather than right through Pontiac, the town has become one of the main stops on the Illinois Route 66 tour, thanks to the presence here of the **Route 66 Association Hall of Fame Museum** (110 W. Howard St., 815/844-4566, daily, free), in the old main fire station. Along with the usual

Welcome to Downtown Pontiac!

displays of gas pumps, enamel and neon advertising signs, and old photos documenting the road's heritage, the Pontiac museum is worth a look for its tribute to iconic Route 66 artist Bob Waldmire (1945-2009), whose delicate line drawings were instrumental in nurturing national enthusiasm for preserving and protecting the unique legacy of Route 66. Many of Bob's drawing and mural paintings and large murals are reproduced here, alongside the 1972 VW camper and the big old Chevy schoolbus RV in which Bob traveled and lived for much of his prolific life. Bob's VW van and his hippy-dippy appreciation of the human and natural history of Route 66 inspired the counter-cultural character "Fillmore" in the movie *Cars*, voiced by comedian George Carlin.

Pontiac is also home to two more excellent attractions. Facing the west side of the landmark Livingston County Courthouse, the world's greatest car museum, officially known as the **Pontiac-Oakland Museum** (815/842-2345, daily, free), displays immaculately preserved Firebirds and Bonnevilles amidst a Smithsonian-worthy array of advertising and related memorabilia, all in a beautifully designed and maintained space reclaimed from a historic showroom. Adding to the aesthetic experience, the small but totally engaging **Wall Dogs Sign and Mural Museum** (815/842-1848, daily, free) is next door. The Wall Dogs are an international collective who get together in places around the world to paint large signs and murals, including most of those adorning the walls of Pontiac buildings.

One more long-lived Route 66 landmark to experience: the **Old Log Cabin Inn** (18700 Old Route 66, 815/842-2908) on the north edge of town. When Route 66 was redirected behind the original location, this restaurant was jacked up and flipped around. The old, old road, which dates from 1918, is still there, behind the café along the railroad tracks.

Bloomington-Normal

Hometown of politician Adlai Stevenson (and Col. Henry Blake of TV's *M*A*S*H*), **Bloomington-Normal** sits at the middle of Illinois, surrounded by five different Interstate freeways and miles of cornfields. Its main claim to fame is in being the only place in the world where that classic bar snack, **Beer Nuts,** is made; for a free sample (but no tour, alas), stop by the **factory** (103 N. Robinson St., 800/BEER-NUTS or 309/827-8580 ext. 324). The "Twin Cities" are also the corporate home of insurance company State Farm and birthplace of another all-American icon, the Midwest-based burger chain Steak 'n Shake, which started here in 1934. Good food is available downtown at **Lucca Grill** (116 E. Market St., 309/828-7521), which has been serving pizza and pasta dishes since the 1930s.

Funks Grove

Heading on from Bloomington-Normal, westbound drivers will encounter the next two towns in sonorous order—Shirley and McLean. Wordplay aside, the stretch of Illinois farmland between Bloomington and Springfield is rich in Route 66-related heritage. In McLean, 47 miles from Springfield and 15 miles southwest from Bloomington, old Route 66 emerges from the shadow of I-55. You can follow old Route 66 along the west side of the freeway for just over four miles past the delightful anachronism of **Funks Grove** (309/874-3360), where the friendly Funk family has been tapping trees and selling delicious maple sirup (that's how they spell it) since 1891. If you're here in late winter or early spring you can watch them tap the trees and hammer in the spouts; each tree can produce up to 4 gallons of sap a day, but it takes 50 gallons of sap for each gallon of the final product. Free tastings are available, and a full range of bottles is on sale.

Lincoln

The only town named for Honest Abe in his lifetime, **Lincoln** (pop. 14,504) took his name before he became a famous figure. As a young lawyer, Abraham Lincoln drew up the legal documents for founding the

Logan County Courthouse in Lincoln

town but warned developers that he "never knew of anything named Lincoln that amounted to much." At the dedication ceremonies, Lincoln supposedly "baptized" the place by spitting out a mouthful of watermelon seeds—hence the plaster watermelon and historical plaque remembering the great event, next to the Amtrak-serviced train station at Broadway and Chicago Streets in the center of town. Lincoln was also home to Harlem Renaissance poet Langston Hughes (1902-1967), who was elected Class Poet while in the 8th grade here.

Springfield

As the Illinois state capital, **Springfield** (pop. 118,033) embodies the rural small-town character of most of the state and feels much farther away from Chicago than the three-plus-hour drive it actually is, traffic willing. Springfield is also the place that takes the "Land of Lincoln" state's obsession with Abraham Lincoln to its greatest extreme, for it was here that Honest Abe worked and lived from 1837 to 1861.

Lincoln's Tomb

He left Springfield after being elected president and was buried here after his assassination at the end of the Civil War.

There are all manner of Lincoln sights to see all over Springfield, but the newest and best place to start your homage is at the state-run **Abraham Lincoln Presidential Library and Museum** (212 N. 6th St., 217/558-8934, daily, $15), across from the Old State Capitol. Once you've toured this comprehensive, reverential yet thought-provoking, over $100 million, 200,000-square-foot complex, other sights include the only home Lincoln ever owned, his law offices, and of course his tomb. Located in Oak Ridge Cemetery, two miles north of downtown, Lincoln's tomb also includes the remains of his wife and three of four children. Legend has it that if you touch the nose on the bronze bust of Lincoln, good luck will follow.

Though quite sincere and understated, the Lincoln homage can overwhelm. If you need a change of pace from Lincoln Land there is the beautiful **Dana-Thomas House** (301 E. Lawrence Ave., 217/782-6776, Wed.-Sun., $10), a half mile south of the state capitol. Designed by Frank Lloyd Wright in 1902, for socialite Susan Dana, who lived here until the late 1940s, it is the most luxurious, best preserved, and most fully furnished of his houses.

Also worth a look is what some say is the oldest gas station on Route 66, **Shea's Gas Station** (2075 Peoria Rd., 217/522-0475). The ever-engaging owner Bill Shea curated a photogenic collection of vintage gasoline pumps,

South of Springfield, on the stretch of old Route 66 that forms the frontage road at I-55 exit 63, near the town of **Raymond,** a marble statue of the Virgin Mary forms a shrine that has become known as **Our Lady of the Highways.**

Parts of the old road survive between Springfield and Litchfield, but the route is incomplete and can be confusing to follow. I-55 makes much shorter work of the 45-mile drive.

signs, shields, and anything else related to the sale and use of our favorite fossil fuel. Sadly, Shea passed away in 2013. While the collection's future is uncertain, it still offers amazing photo-ops, even from the outside.

Springfield also has a favorite Route 66 watering hole, the **Cozy Dog Drive-In** (2935 S. 6th St., 217/525-1992), on the old road south of downtown. The birthplace of the corn dog, which here goes by the nicer name "Cozy," was founded in 1949 by Ed Waldmire, father of noted Route 66 artist Bob Waldmire. So come on in and chow down—two Cozy Dogs, a cold drink, and a big basket of fries cost around $9.

Complete your Route 66 Americana tour by taking in a flick or two at the **Route 66 Twin Drive-In** (1700 Recreation Dr., 217/698-0066), west of Sixth Street southwest of the I-72/I-55 junction.

Almost all the national chain hotels and motels have operations in Springfield, so you shouldn't have trouble finding a room. For Victorian character in a convenient location, consider the elegant **Pasfield House Inn** (525 S. Pasfield St., 217/525-3663, $125 and up).

Litchfield and Mount Olive

Between Springfield and Cahokia Mounds, the most interesting stretch of old Route 66 runs along the east side of the freeway for about a dozen miles, between Litchfield and Mount Olive. First stop is **Litchfield,** an old coal-mining center that is home to one of the best and most stylish Route 66 restaurants, the **Ariston Café** (413 N. Old Route 66, 217/324-2023, Tues.-Sun.), right in the heart of town at the junction of old Route 66 and Hwy-16. The food is a step or two up from the usual roadside fare, and the white linen and refined decor have earned it a spot in the Route 66 Hall of Fame. The rest of Litchfield reeks of the old road, with cafés, motor courts, and old billboards aplenty, plus another old "ozoner," the **Sky View Drive-In** (217/324-4451) on old Route 66 one mile north of town.

Some seven miles southwest of Litchfield, the hamlet of **Mount Olive** (pop. 2,052) was a bustling coal-mining center in the early 20th century. It's now a sleepy little community, where the only signs of its mining past are in the Union Miners Cemetery, along old Route 66 at the northwest edge of town. Near the rear is a granite shaft rising from an elaborate pedestal, which serves as a memorial to Mary Harris "Mother" Jones (1830?-1930), the celebrated union activist (and namesake of the liberal-minded magazine) who was famous for her passionate oratory, like the phrase "Pray for the dead, and fight like hell for the living." She died here, possibly aged 100, while supporting a miners' strike, and is buried nearby. Her grave is marked by a simple headstone.

For old-road fans, Mount Olive is also home to the oldest surviving service station on Route 66, the immaculate, restored (but no longer in business) Shell station downtown, long owned by Russell Soulsby.

Collinsville: Cahokia Mounds

Old Route 66 followed today's I-270 around the north side of St. Louis, crossing the Mississippi River on the restored Chain of Rocks Bridge, but one of southern Illinois's biggest attractions sits directly east of the Gateway Arch, off the I-55/70 freeway at exit 6. Clearly visible to the south side of the Interstate, the enigmatic humps of **Cahokia Mounds State Historic Site** are the remains of the largest prehistoric Indian city north of Mexico. Over 100 earthen mounds of various sizes were built here by the indigenous Mississippian culture while Europe was in the Dark Ages. The largest covers 14 acres—more ground than the Great Pyramid of Cheops. But don't expect the works of the pharaohs: Symmetrical, grass-covered hills sitting in flat, lightly wooded bottomlands are what you'll find here. The view of the Gateway Arch in distant St. Louis from the 100-foot top of Monks Mound lends an odd sense of grandeur to the site. A sophisticated **Interpretive Center** (618/346-5160, hours vary) is a recommended first stop for its exhibits, award-winning multimedia orientation show, and guided and self-guided tours.

The nearest town to the Cahokia Mounds is **Collinsville,** a pleasant little place that's nearly world-famous for its

The Cahokia Mounds sit in the middle of the American Bottom, a floodplain whose gunpowder-black alluvial soils have long been considered among the richest and most productive in the world. However, Charles Dickens called it an "ill-favored Black Hollow" after enduring its mud, which, as he wrote in *American Notes,* had "no variety but in depth."

170-foot-high **World's Largest Catsup Bottle,** which rises high above Hwy-159 a half mile south of Main Street, on the grounds of what used to be the **Brooks Catsup Company** (800 S. Morrison Ave.). This decorated water tower was constructed in 1949 and restored by the people of Collinsville in 1993; it has since been adopted by Collinsville as a super-size symbol of local pride and perseverance.

Chain of Rocks Bridge

If you have the time and the inclination to stretch your legs and breath deeply, make your way to the northeast edge of St. Louis, where instead of following the 75-mph I-270 freeway, you can cross the Mississippi between Illinois and Missouri on the historic **Chain of Rocks Bridge.** The bridge has been renovated for use as a mile-long **bike and hiking trail** (314/416-9930, daylight hours only), decorated with an array of old gas pumps and signs, just south of the modern I-270 freeway. If you're driving, the best parking is on the Illinois side of the bridge, but cyclists or energetic walkers can cross the surprisingly narrow bridge and continue all the way to the Gateway Arch in St. Louis, following an 11-mile Riverfront Trail that snakes between the flood walls, the river, and acres of heavy (and sometimes smelly) industry.

Not quite on the same scale as the Cahokia Mounds, the Chain of Rocks Bridge, or even the Collinsville catsup bottle, the nearby Route 66 town of **Mitchell** holds one more Route 66 landmark: 85-year-old **Luna Café** (201 E. Chain of Rocks Rd., 618/931-3152), a one-time casino, speakeasy, and brothel that's now a pretty seedy but very "atmospheric" bar, north of the I-270 freeway exit 6, along old Route 66.

MISSOURI

The Ozark Highlands of southern Missouri, which Route 66 crosses in its 300-odd-mile journey between Illinois and Kansas, are about the only significant hills the road crosses east of the Sandia Mountains in New Mexico. This plateau region, though not by any means alpine or breathtaking, is visually dynamic in a way the broad flatlands of Illinois or Oklahoma rarely are. Though the I-44 freeway has replaced the old road all the way across the state, there are many signs of older alignments, and just about every Interstate exit drops you within a moment's drive of the Mother Road. Missouri also holds some great old motels and one of the greatest of the old Route 66 tourist attractions—**Meramec Caverns,** an extensive set of limestone caves offering the most over-the-top underground tour you can take.

Route 66 Across St. Louis

It can be maddening to follow old Route 66 across St. Louis, but its many great spots—Ted Drewes Frozen Custard Stand, in particular—make it well worth the effort. One route crossed the Mississippi River right into downtown from Collinsville, Illinois, while another "City 66" route headed across the Chain of Rocks Bridge before running into downtown St. Louis along Florissant Avenue and Riverview Drive.

Heading southwest out of downtown, the old road followed Gravois Avenue, Chippewa Street, and Watson Road, just south of the parallel I-44 freeway.

Times Beach: Route 66 State Park

There's no plaque or notice proudly marking the spot, but the story of **Times Beach** (pop. 0) deserves mention. Founded in the 1920s as a weekend getaway a dozen miles west of St. Louis along the Meramec River, the town grew into a working-class commuter suburb, with some 2,000 people, thanks to Route 66. But there were no paved streets except for the not-yet-famous highway that passed through the center of town. Times Beach remained a quiet

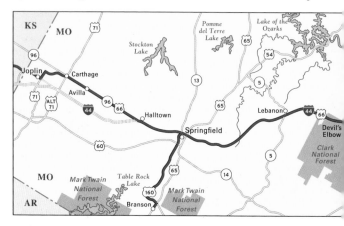

hamlet until 1982, when the federal government discovered that the industrial oil sprayed on streets to keep down dust had in fact been contaminated with toxic dioxin. The toxic waste, combined with a Meramec River flood that buried the town for over a week, made Times Beach uninhabitable.

In 1984 the government paid $33 million to buy Times Beach and tear it down, and 15 years later the cleanup was declared complete. Four hundred acres of what was once Times Beach have since been reopened as the **Route 66 State Park** (636/938-7198, daily, free), north of I-44 exits 265 and 266, with hiking trails, river access, and a nice little museum on Times Beach and Route 66, housed in a 1930s roadhouse.

Eureka and Gray Summit: I-44

Heading south and west out of St. Louis, the I-44 freeway has pretty well obliterated old Route 66 as far as **Eureka,** where the sprawling amusement park **Six Flags St. Louis** (636/938-5300, around $60) effectively marks the city's suburban edge. The park has all the thrill rides and water park fun you could want, and often hosts concerts and special events.

A very different experience can be had at **Gray Summit,** just west of Six Flags, where the Missouri Botanical Garden tends to the magical **Shaw Nature Reserve** (636/451-3512, daily, $5), a 2,400-acre

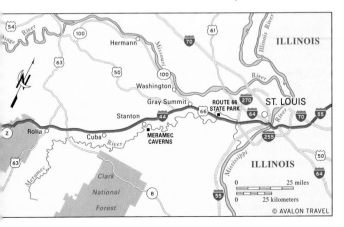

St. Louis

the Gateway Arch

Founded by French fur trappers in 1764, St. Louis served for most of its first century as a prosperous outpost of "civilization" at the frontier of the Wild West. It was the starting point for the explorations of Lewis and Clark, and much later Charles Lindbergh, whose *Spirit of St. Louis* carried him across the Atlantic. Unfortunately, like many other American cities, St. Louis has suffered from years of decline and neglect; the population, which peaked at over 850,000 in 1950, is now less than half that, and the sale of the city's iconic beer, Budweiser, to the Belgian company InBev didn't exactly thrill many locals. Although it has all the cultural and institutional trappings of a major city, not to mention the landmark Gateway Arch, St. Louis is at heart a city of small neighborhoods, such as bluesy Soulard south of downtown, the Italian-American "Hill" (boyhood home of Yogi Berra), and the collegiate West End district near verdant Forest Park.

One thing you have to see when in St. Louis (you literally cannot miss it) is the **Gateway Arch** (daily, 314/655-1600), on the riverfront at the foot of Market Street. Rising up from the west bank of the Mississippi River, Eero Saarinen's stunning 630-foot stainless steel monument still dominates the city skyline, despite the disrespectful rise of nearby office towers. Under the legs of the arch, which is officially called the Jefferson National Expansion Memorial, the free and fascinating **Museum of Westward Expansion** chronicles the human wave that swept America's frontier west to the Pacific. A small elevator-like **tram** ($10) carries visitors up the arch to an observation chamber at the very top.

West of downtown around the Washington University campus, in **Forest Park**'s 1,300 beautifully landscaped acres, museums of fine art, history, and science fill buildings that date back to the 1904 World's Fair, St. Louis's world-class swan song.

The **St. Louis Cardinals** (314/345-9600), one of the country's most popular baseball teams, play at retro-modern **Busch Stadium,** right downtown with views of the river and Gateway Arch. Games are broadcast on **KMOX 1120 AM.**

PRACTICALITIES

Freeways and high-speed arteries reminiscent of Los Angeles make a car handy for navigating the St. Louis area—unless you have oodles of money for cab fares. Thanks to the city's sad history of replacing its landmark buildings with blacktop, you'll find plenty of parking lots around downtown.

For food, The Hill neighborhood is hard to beat: **Gian-Tony's** (5356 Daggett Ave., 314/772-4893) is perhaps the best of a dozen classic neighborhood Italian places. Wherever you go, try the toasted ravioli, a local treat. Near Washington University, another great place is the slightly kitschy **Blueberry Hill** (6504 Delmar Blvd., 314/727-4444), a retro-1950s diner that has an excellent jukebox, very good burgers, and enough real-life credibility to sometimes attract the likes of St. Louis-born father of rock 'n' roll, Chuck Berry, to play impromptu gigs.

No one leaves St. Louis without cruising old Route 66 southwest from downtown to **Ted Drewes** (6726 Chippewa Ave., 314/481-2652), a local institution famous for its many flavors of "concrete"—a delicious frozen dairy-and-egg-custard concoction so thick you can turn it upside down and not spill a drop. Nearby, fried chicken fans flock to **Hodak's** (2100 Gravois Ave., 314/776-7292). One last Route 66 place has been going strong for more than 60 years: the **Eat-Rite Diner** (622 Chouteau Ave., 314/621-9651), a plain blue-and-white cube serving up breakfasts and burgers 24 hours daily. As the sign says: "Eat Rite, or Don't Eat at All."

St. Louis doesn't have that much of a tourist trade (the muggy weather here in summer keeps most sensible people far away), so places to stay are relatively cheap. **Hampton Inn at Gateway Arch** (333 Washington Ave., 314/621-7900, $99 and up) is one of the more popular downtown hotels. The **Hyatt Regency at the Arch** (315 Chestnut St., 314/655-1234, $129 and up) is another. In a historic rein-

carnation, a quartet of stately old warehouses has been converted to house the **Westin St. Louis** (811 Spruce St., 314/621-2000, $200 and up), near the arch, the river, and the baseball stadium.

semi-wilderness of native plants, cultivated orchards, and wildflower meadows, just 40 miles from the Gateway Arch. And if you like animals, especially dogs and cats, you'll want to check out the well-trained pets showcased across I-44 at **Purina Farms** (314/982-3232, Tues.-Sun. 9:30am-4pm summer, Wed.-Fri. 9:30am-3pm and Sat.-Sun. 9:30am-4pm spring and fall, free). Dogs catch Frisbees and do all sorts of amazing tricks, while cats sit there and look pretty.

In between Six Flags and the Shaw Nature Reserve, Route 66 re-emerges from the shadows of I-44, winding through the hamlet of **Pacific,** where the Red Cedar Inn served dinner every evening from 1935 to 2007, when it closed. West of Pacific, Route 66 climbs toward Gray Summit past the faded old Route 66 sign for the Diamonds Truck Stop and the Gardenway Motel.

For most of the 30 miles between Gray Summit and Meramec Caverns, old Route 66 is overwhelmed by the I-44 freeway, so most Route 66 aficionados opt for the freeway and save their exploring for better stretches, like Devil's Elbow.

Meramec Caverns

The best stop along old Route 66's trek across Missouri, and one of the most enjoyable and charming roadside attractions along the entire Mother Road, **Meramec Caverns** (573/468-2283, daily, $20) is a set of limestone caves advertised by signs on barns and buildings all along the route, and all over the Midwest. First developed during the Civil War, when the natural saltpeter was mined for use in manufacturing gunpowder, the caves were later popularized as a place for local farmers to get together for dances. The largest room in the caves is still used for Easter

Among its many other claims to fame, Meramec Caverns is known as the birthplace of the bumper sticker.

Meramec Caverns: nature's best sculpture and a disco light show!

DETOUR: BRANSON

A middle-American mecca, mixing equal parts Las Vegas glitz and Myrtle Beach summer fun, Branson is a century-old Ozark resort town that hit the big time in the 1980s through clever promotion and cunning repackaging of country-and-Western music and God-fearing recreation. There are well over 50 major performance venues in Branson, and looking down the list of luminaries who have played here—the Osmond Brothers, Tony Orlando, and Jim "I Don't Like Spiders and Snakes" Stafford—you'd think that anyone who had a hit record or a TV show, or can still sing and smile at the same time, can have their own showcase theater. To cater to the estimated 7 million annual visitors, the range of shows keeps expanding, at times including such exotic offerings as Acrobats of China or the Beatles-themed Liverpool Legends.

What originally put Branson on the tourist map was not music but a book: *The Shepherd of the Hills*, by Harold Bell Wright. Set in and around Branson and published in 1907, it was a huge best-seller, with a hugely complicated plot. Adapted in the 1930s into an outdoor **stage play** (800/653-6288, $37), featuring more than 80 actors if not quite a cast of thousands, *Shepherd of the Hills* has been drawing visitors to Branson ever since.

Entertainment aside, the Ozark Mountains area around Branson is still a lovely place to explore; just about any road south, east, or west will take you through beautifully scenic mountain landscapes. And if scenery is not enough, one of the most popular spots in Branson is **Silver Dollar City** (800/475-9370 or 417/336-7100, daily, $59 and up), nine miles west of Branson via Hwy-76, a turn-of-the-20th-century theme park devoted to Ozark arts, crafts, and music—and roller coasters.

services, arts and crafts shows, and even the occasional chamber of commerce meeting. An hour west of St. Louis, Meramec Caverns was opened as a tourist attraction in 1935 by Lester Dill, who guided visitors through the elaborate chambers and, more importantly, was a true master of the art of garnering cheap but effective publicity for his tourist attraction. An example: After World War II, Dill sent his son-in-law to the top of the Empire State Building dressed up as a caveman and had him threaten to jump off unless everyone in the world visited Meramec Caverns.

Fact and fiction mix freely at Meramec Caverns, adding to the pleasures of seeing the massive caves. Jesse James used these caverns as a hideout, and at least once took advantage of the underground river to escape through the secret "back door." Though Meramec is not huge compared to other caves, the natural formations are among the most sculptural and delicate of any cave you can visit, and the man-made additions are all low-tech and kitschy

white hawthorn,
state flower of Missouri

enough to be charming. The hand-operated sound-and-light show ends with a grand finale of Kate Smith singing "God Bless America," while the red, white, and blue of Old Glory is projected onto a limestone curtain. For the full Meramec experience, add in a canoe ride or a zip-wire ride, or stay the night in the pleasant riverside campground.

Meramec Caverns is near the town of **Stanton,** 55 miles west of St. Louis, 3 miles south of I-44 exit 230. There's a small café and a motel on the grounds, which spread along the banks of the Meramec River. At the I-44 exit, the odd little **Jesse James Wax Museum** (573/927-5233, daily June-Aug., weekends only Apr.-May and Sept.-Oct., closed Nov.-Mar., $7) insists, despite all evidence to the contrary, that a 100-year-old man who turned up in Stanton in 1948 was in fact Jesse James.

Cuba

Along I-44 west of Meramec Caverns, the old Route 66 roadside is lined by ramshackle wooden stands, which, toward the end of summer, sell sweet Concord grapes from local Rosati vineyards. The stands are located along the frontage roads (which in many cases are the remnants of the original Route 66), but people park along the freeway and walk to them. At the eastern edge of this grape-growing district, the small town of **Cuba** has a vintage Phillips 66 gas station and a dozen colorful murals covering large areas of downtown buildings with scenes from Cuba's history (depicting everything from the Civil War to the day in 1928 when Amelia Earhart made an emergency landing in a farmer's field).

Cuba also makes it onto many Route 66 itineraries thanks to the friendly **Wagon Wheel Motel** (901 E. Washington St., 573/885-3411, $60 and up), which for many years was famous for offering 1930s charm at 1970s prices. Although it's been remodeled, the Wagon Wheel still allows travelers to sample a kinder, gentler, less complicated era—even while taking advantage of clean comfy beds and free Wi-Fi. The Wagon Wheel Motel is right on Route 66. An added bonus: good barbecue is right next door at the **Missouri Hick BBQ** (573/885-6791).

The route west from Cuba to Rolla, along what's now marked as Hwy-ZZ, offers a fine stretch of unsullied Route 66 scenery, made all the more enticing by the presence of the **World's Largest Rocker,** a Guinness-sanctioned champion chair (not a musician!) standing more than 40 feet tall, 4 miles west of Cuba outside the Fanning Outpost souvenir stand and archery supply store.

Rolla

Twenty miles west of Cuba, about midway between St. Louis and Springfield, one of the liveliest towns along the Ozark Mountains stretch of Route 66 is **Rolla** (pop. 18,488; pronounced "RAW-la"). In the center of town, right along old Route 66 on the campus of the Missouri University of Science and Technology (MUST), one big draw is the half-scale replica of that ancient Druidical observatory, **Stonehenge,** created in 1984 to show off the high-tech stone carving capabilities of MUST's High Pressure Water Jet Lab. If you have trouble finding Rolla's Stonehenge, this miniature Wonder of the World stands across Route 66 from the **Great Wall** (1505 N. Bishop Ave., 573/341-9922), a pretty good Chinese restaurant. Talk about "small world."

Adding to the surprising mix of international flavors is another Rolla tradition: a wild and crazy St. Patrick's Day party, held every year since 1908, during which students paint the streets of Rolla green, slay rubber snakes, and drink just about anything they can find, all in homage to the Emerald Isle.

Amongst the I-44 freeway clutter of Waffle Houses and Shoney's at the west end of Rolla, there's still a sign for the fireworks and moccasins on sale at the landmark **Totem Pole Trading Post—since 1933.** Once you've got your fill of T-shirts and postcards, head up the hill to Rolla's most popular watering hole, **Joe and Linda's Tater Patch** (103 Bridge School Rd., 573/368-3111). It's on the south side of Route 66 across from the Rolla visitors center. Try one of their signature baked potatoes topped with pulled pork for a unique taste treat. They've also been serving big breakfasts, pork tenderloins, delicious onion rings, and ice-cold beer for more than 40 years.

Old Route 66: Devil's Elbow

West of Rolla towards Springfield, I-44 has been built right on top of the old Route 66 corridor. Dozens of mostly abandoned old motels, motor courts, gas stations, and other highway-dependent businesses line the remains of the old road, which still serves as a freeway frontage road for most of the way. There are plenty of antiques shops and cafés to make detours interesting, and the longish detour along old Route 66 through the **Devil's Elbow** district is especially memorable. But if you're pressed for time, even the Interstate superslab offers a plenty-scenic drive through these upland Ozark Mountains, much of which are protected from development within the Mark Twain National Forest.

This is the most ruggedly picturesque stretch of Route 66 across Missouri; the name "Devil's Elbow" comes from a section of the Big Piney River that turns so acutely it caused repeated logjams. The earliest incarnations of Route 66 followed what's now signed as "Teardrop Road," and up until 1981 the last alignment of Route 66 followed what's now the very hilly, four-lane **Hwy-Z**, some of the last Missouri sections of the old road to be bypassed by I-44 (all this is between I-44 exits 163 and 169).

Besides the old road itself, a great reason to tour this 10-mile stretch of old Route 66 is the chance to sample some fine Missouri barbecue at the **Elbow Inn** (573/336-5375), just south of the junction of Hwy-Z and Teardrop Road, a lively, good-natured biker bar with cans of cold beer and lots of bras pinned to the ceiling. If you're a barbecue fan, you can vote for mid-Missouri's best ribs by comparing the Elbow Inn with its nearest competitor, the **Sweetwater BBQ** (573/336-8830), on Hwy-Z just southeast of I-44 exit 163.

West of here, the scenic old road crashes suddenly back into the franchised fast food of I-44 at the twin towns of St. Robert and Waynesville, where 30,000-plus soldiers and dependents at the nearby Fort Leonard Wood U.S. Army base, headquarters of the U.S. Army military police school (and a small museum), have generated a rash of Wal-Marts and shopping malls.

Lebanon: Munger Moss

The stretch of old Route 66 running through **Lebanon** (pop. 14,292) holds more than its fair share of sights, so make sure you slow down and soak it all in. The most worthwhile but easiest-to-

miss sight is the excellent **Route 66 Museum** (915 S. Jefferson St., 417/532-2148), tucked away inside the Lebanon/Laclede County Public Library, next door to the Ritz 8 Cineplex. Here the whole history of the U.S. highway systems is conveyed through maps, postcards, promotional posters, and life-size dioramas. The stretch of old Route 66 running from the museum along the north side of I-44 holds the marvelous **Munger Moss Motel** (1336 E. Route 66, 417/532-3111, $45), where Ramona Lehman and family have been offering clean rooms, a swimming pool, and a wonderful neon sign since 1946. Across from the Munger Moss is a bowling alley with a snack bar and a set of batting cages (5 cents a pitch!), making it a perfect Route 66 destination.

Follow Elm Street (old Route 66) east from downtown Lebanon,

past the Munger Moss and along the north side of I-44 to two more highlights. On weekend nights, noisy NASCAR stock cars race around the asphalt oval of the **Lebanon Speedway** (417/532-2060, $10). Just beyond the track, at I-44 exit 135, there's another nice surprise: **Mr. C's Routepost** (24200 Route 66,_ 417/588-4466), an above-average souvenir stand with the exceptional collection of Chicago Blues memorabilia personally assembled by its owner, Scott "Mr. C" Cameron, longtime manager of Muddy Waters and Willie Dixon.

Detour:
The Laura Ingalls Wilder Museum

While the good food and warm Munger Moss hospitality is more than reason enough to visit Lebanon, the town also marks the turnoff for a trip to visit another American institution, the Ozark Mountain homestead where author Laura Ingalls Wilder wrote the famous *Little House* books. Though it's an hour detour south via Hwy-5, or 45 miles due east of Springfield via US-60, Wilder's

Rocky Ridge Farm has been preserved as the **Laura Ingalls Wilder Home and Museum** (3068 Hwy. A, 877/924-7126, daily Mar. 1-Nov. 15, $10), on a hill 2 miles southeast of the town of Mansfield. Unlike the many reconstructed Little House sights elsewhere, this museum has a direct and intimate connection with the woman who, for generations of readers, brought the American frontier to life. Born in 1867, Wilder grew up with the country, her iconic "little house" moving ever westwards from the "big woods" of Wisconsin on to the "prairie" of Kansas and South Dakota. Wilder moved to the Ozarks in 1894 and worked to establish a successful apple and dairy farm. It was not until the economic downturns of the 1930s, when Wilder was in her 60s, that she began publishing her books, which have since sold millions (some of the royalties go to support the Mansfield library, where there is also a small museum). The home the Wilders lived in most of their adult lives forms the heart of the museum. They are buried in the town cemetery, alongside their daughter Rose, who urged on (and some say collaborated on) Laura's autobiographical stories.

Springfield

The largest city in southern Missouri, **Springfield** (pop. 157,630) doesn't feel nearly as big as it is, though it does sprawl for many miles in all directions. Despite the ongoing growth and development, most notably the green and pleasant **Jordan Valley Park** sur-

rounding the attractive downtown baseball stadium and sports complex, Springfield has preserved much of its old Route 66 frontage, along St. Louis Street east of downtown, as well as the grandly named Chestnut Expressway west of downtown. The 20-mph speed limit on downtown streets—along with tons of free parking—enables Route 66 pilgrims to pay homage to the town's Arabesque landmark **Shrine Mosque theater** (601 E. Saint Louis St.), which still hosts occasional concerts.

Springfield is also celebrated as the place where "Wild Bill" Hickok killed fellow gambler Dave Tutt, apparently because Tutt wore the watch he'd won from Hickok playing cards. A plaque in the central square, just west of the Shrine Mosque, tells one of many variations on the tale.

Springfield has at least one fine old Route 66 motel: the **Route 66 Rail Haven** (203 S. Glenstone Ave., 417/866-1963 or 800/304-0021, $70 and up), on the corner of old Route 66 and US-65. Open since 1938, it has been fully modernized and now is a Best Western affiliate with a railroad theme. A mile away on old Route 66 is one of the earliest and most stylish models of the **Steak 'n Shake** burger chain (1158 St. Louis St., 417/866-6109); open 24 hours, this is one of the last ones where carhops still bring your food to your car (during daylight hours).

Springfield is home to the Double-A Texas League **Springfield Cardinals,** who play off US-65 at one of the country's most attractive ballparks, **Hammons Field** (417/863-2143).

A great stretch of old Route 66, renumbered Hwy-96, runs for 50 miles along the north side of I-44 between Springfield and Carthage, passing rolling pastures and little towns like Halltown and Avilla, with antiques shops and abandoned cafés lining the old highway frontage.

Carthage

Just shy of the Kansas border, six miles north of I-44 and right on old Route 66, **Carthage** (pop. 14,378) is a perfect little town, looking for all the world like the model for the idyllic-though-fictional town of Hill Valley from the *Back to the Future* movies. The center of Carthage, three blocks south of Route 66, is dominated by the outrageously ornate, circa-1895, limestone **Jasper County Courthouse,** which features a local history mural and an open-cage elevator in the lobby. (On Thursdays and Fridays the elevator is hand-operated by a charming and friendly woman, Geraldine Bunn, who serves as Carthage's unofficial ambassador.)

Across the street from the courthouse there's a good place to eat: the **Carthage Deli** (301 S. Main St., 417/358-8820, closed Sun.), which serves sandwiches and milk shakes in a 1950s-style soda fountain on the northwest corner of the courthouse square. Two blocks east is a bowling alley, **Star Lanes** (219 E. 3rd St., 417/358-2144). Also in Carthage is an old Route 66 landmark: the glowing pink-and-green 1940s neon sign of the **Boots Motel** (107 S. Garrison St., 417/310-2989, $72) welcomed Clark Gable and hundreds of other weary travelers over the years. Local preservationists and Route 66 fans had renovated the property and reopened a few rooms for retro-minded overnight guests.

Carthage was the boyhood home of naturalist Marlin Perkins, host of Mutual of Omaha's *Wild Kingdom* TV show. A life-sized statue of him stands in Central Park, three blocks southwest of the courthouse square. Carthage was also the girlhood home of Wild West outlaw Belle Starr.

A mile or so west of downtown on Old Route 66, enjoy a double feature of Hollywood blockbusters in the comfort of your car at the **66 Drive-In** (17231 Old 66 Blvd., 417/359-5959, weekends only).

Finally, if you have a soft spot for hyperbolic sentimentality, don't miss the **Precious Moments Chapel** (800/543-7975, daily, free), featuring the wide-eyed characters from the religious figurine series. The chapel is well signed, west of US-71 on the southwest edge of Carthage.

Joplin

About 16 miles southeast of Joplin, **George Washington Carver National Monument** (417/325-4151, daily, free) preserves the farm where the eminent agricultural scientist, educator, and self-sufficiency advocate grew up in the 1860s.

If you want to travel the old Route 66 alignment across Kansas, you'll also pass through **Joplin** (pop. 50,15), a border town that's the industrial center of the tri-state region. Formerly a lead- and zinc-mining town, in May 2011 Joplin made the national news in the worst possible way when it was hit by one of the most powerful tornados in recent U.S. history, 200-mph winds tearing a swath of destruction and killing more than 150 people in less than 10 minutes of terror. Before the tornado, Joplin was better known for its high-quality limestone quarries than for its history, though highway heritage is well served at **Schifferdecker Park,** west of downtown off 7th Street, a pre-Route 66 rest area that now has a mining museum, small historical museum, and a public **swimming pool** (417/625-4750, daily, $5) that is much appreciated on a sweltering late summer day. Though the tornado destroyed dozens of homes and businesses, Joplin's downtown area does hold one unlikely attraction, a vibrant mural by artist Thomas Hart Benton depicting life in Joplin at the turn of the 20th century. The over-70-square-foot mural, which turned out to be the artist's final complete work, is in the

Massive lead mines like this have disappeared from Kansas.

lobby of the **Joplin City Hall** (602 S. Main St.).

Joplin has a number of good places to eat. Try the excellent BBQ at **Big R's** (1220 E. 15th St., 417/781-5959). The smoky brisket and juicy ribs make it hard to leave room for the tasty pies. The popular **Eagle Drive-In** (4244 S. Main St., 417/623-2228) has a wide range of burgers, veggie burgers, and daily specials.

On the Kansas/Missouri border, tune to **KXMS 88.7** for classical music.

KANSAS

The shortest but perhaps best-signed stretch of Route 66's eight-state run is its 13.2-mile slice across the southeast corner of Kansas. Be careful not to blink your eyes, or you'll be saying, as Dorothy did in *The Wizard of Oz,* "I have a feeling we're not in Kansas anymore."

Coming from Missouri, your first town in Kansas is **Galena,** where the funky **Galena Mining and Historical Museum** (319 W. 7th St., 620/783-2192, hours vary), just off the main drag and marked by a big Old 66 sign, is stuffed with old newspaper clippings and other items that give a glimpse of town life during its 1920s-era mining heyday. At its peak, Galena had a population near 30,000 (10 times the current number). Various rusting tools and machines testify to the work that once went on here. That said, the hospitable Route 66 spirit lives on, most obviously at **Cars on the Route** (119 N. Main St., 620/783-1366), inside the old Kan-O-Tex gas station, now serving sandwiches and selling souvenirs related to Pixar's animated Route 66 movie *Cars.* The early 1950s International Harvester tow truck that apparently inspired the *Cars* character "Tow Mater" is parked outside.

Another appetizing attraction awaits in **Riverton,** the next town to the west, where the **Old Riverton Store** (7109 SE Hwy. 66, 620/848-3330), a.k.a. "Eisler Brothers," has been open since the 1920s. Across the highway from a big power plant, the old store has a good deli counter, with very good handmade sandwiches. The last of the Eislers passed away in 2009, but the store is still in good hands, headquarters of the small but active Kansas Route 66 Association, and an essential stop for fans of the old road.

Heading west towards Oklahoma, the newer highway bypasses a fine old rainbow-arched Route 66 concrete bridge, well-signed on the northeast side of **Baxter Springs.** Locals point with pride at the circa-1870 **Crowell Bank** in the historic three-block downtown, which was said to have been robbed by Jesse James. A block away, the nicely restored 1930s Phillips 66 filling station is now a useful museum and Baxter Springs **information center** (620/856-2066) at 10th Street and Military Avenue (a.k.a. Route 66).

Though it's pretty quiet these days, during the Civil War Baxter Springs saw one of the worst massacres in the country's history, when more than 100 unarmed Union soldiers, including many African Americans, were captured and killed by William Quantrill's rebel Confederate raiders (including the aforementioned Jesse James), who had disguised themselves by wearing blue Union uniforms. A monument to the murdered soldiers stands in **Baxter Springs Soldiers' Lot** in the Baxter City Cemetery, off US-166 two miles west of town.

While the soda fountain is no more, this enticing sign remains.

Baxter Springs information center

OKLAHOMA

Apart from occasional college football teams, Oklahoma doesn't often get to crow about being the best in the country, but as far as Route 66 is concerned, the state is definitely number one. Containing more still-drivable miles of the old highway than any other state, Oklahoma is definitely mecca for old-roads fans.

The Dust Bowl exodus of the 1930s uprooted thousands of families who headed west on Route 66, and today many of the towns along the road take bittersweet pride in their *The Grapes of Wrath* connections.

You can also still see signs that go back further into the state's history, just over a century ago, when all of Oklahoma was Indian Territory. It was the last refuge of Kiowa, Apache, Comanche, and other tribes before the U.S. government took even this land away from them during "land rushes" in the 1890s. Today, some tribes have retained enough legal autonomy to issue license plates and run casinos.

Oklahoma has the longest and most intact stretches of old Route 66. If you really want to explore it to the full, get your hands on a copy of the essential map-packed road guide *Oklahoma Route 66,* by Arcadia, Oklahoma's own Jim Ross.

Northeast Oklahoma: The Sidewalk Highway

In the far northeastern corner of Oklahoma, old Route 66 runs through a hardscrabble former lead- and zinc-mining region, from the Kansas border to Vinita on the I-44 Turnpike. Three miles southwest of the Kansas border, **Quapaw** could be the first or last Oklahoma town you visit, depending upon your direction, but either way it's worth a look for the many murals painted on the walls of downtown businesses. The next town along, **Commerce** (pop. 2,473), was another old mining town, noteworthy as the boyhood home of the late, great Yankee switch-hitter Mickey Mantle, in whose honor the old Route 66 alignment down Main Street has been renamed. A statue of Mantle graces the Commerce high school baseball field, right off Route 66.

Four miles to the south via old Route 66 (now signed as US-69), **Miami** holds the magnificent Spanish Revival-style Coleman Theater, built in 1929 when the town was still luxuriating in the riches coming out of the surrounding mines.

old-style Conoco station, Commerce

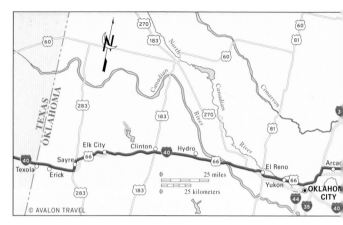

Still following US-69, now roughly parallel to (and eventually crossing under) I-44 between Miami and Afton, some of the earliest paved stretches of old Route 66 were constructed only one lane wide, because in 1926 the state of Oklahoma did not have enough money to build a full-width version. Not surprisingly, these lengths of the road became known as the **"Sidewalk Highway."** The easiest stretch to find runs parallel to US-69: Turn west at the Northeast Technology Center vocational school along an increasingly narrow country lane, and look out for the 66 shields painted on the pavement. This "Sidewalk Highway" rejoins the main Route 66 alignment at Afton, where a convenience store now stands on the site of the fabled Buffalo Ranch Trading Post. For more on Afton, the Buffalo Ranch, Route 66, or help finding the Sidewalk Highway, head down to **Afton Station** (12 SW 1st St., 918/257-4044), a nicely renovated 1930s-era gas station that has been brought back to life as a gift shop and museum of mostly old Packard cars.

Vinita

Old Route 66 crosses the Interstate (a.k.a. the Will Rogers Turnpike) again at **Vinita,** where the region's Native American heritage is brought into focus at the **Eastern Trails Museum** (215 W. Illinois St., 918/256-2115, hours vary, free), next to the public library. The exhibits center on the Cherokee Trail of Tears, which brought the tribe here after a forced march from North Carolina in the 1830s, but the museum also covers the general history of the surrounding area.

Vinita is home to the **Will Rogers Memorial Rodeo,** held here each August since 1935, the year he died. Rogers attended secondary school

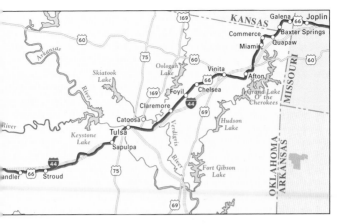

in Vinita after growing up near Claremore. Vinita also hosts the annual **World's Largest Calf Fry Festival and Cook-Off** in late June. (Calf
fries are prairie oysters, otherwise known as beef testicles. Just so you
know.) Contact the **visitors center** (918/256-7133) for details on any
of these.

Vinita also has a great old Route 66 restaurant: **Clanton's Cafe**
(319 E. Illinois Ave., 918/256-9053), right at the center of town.
"Oklahoma's oldest family-owned and -operated restaurant,"
Clanton's has been famous for its chick-
en-fried beefsteak, served here with
mashed potatoes and slathered in pep-
pery white gravy, since 1927. Clanton's
also has good burgers and, in case you
miss the festival, calf fries. (See above
for a disclaimer.)

Foyil

Between Vinita and Claremore, old
Route 66 survives in regular use as the
"free road" alternative to the I-44
Turnpike, alternating between two-lane
and divided four-lane highway. The
most interesting wide spot along this
stretch of hallowed road is **Foyil,** where in the 1940s and 1950s retired fiddle-maker and folk artist Ed Galloway sculpted an outdoor
garden of giant totem poles—the tallest is over 90 feet—and other
Native American-inspired objects out of concrete. After fading and
weathering for many years, the poles, four miles east of town via

Foyil was the hometown
of Andy Payne, the
Cherokee youth who in
1928 won the "Bunion
Derby," a coast-to-coast
foot race that followed
Route 66 from Los
Angeles to Chicago, then
headed east to New York
City—equivalent to
running a marathon and
a half every day for the 84
days it took him to finish.

Totem Pole Park

Hwy-28A, were restored in 1993-1994 as **Totem Pole Park** (918/342-1169 and 918/342-9149, daily dawn-dusk, free). It's now a fascinating place to stop for a picnic or to simply admire the effort that went into these "Watts Towers of the Plains."

Claremore: Will Rogers Memorial

Twenty miles northeast of Tulsa, **Claremore** (pop. 18,581) is a bigger-than-average Route 66 town, one that will be forever connected with its favorite son, Will Rogers (1879-1935). Rogers was born nearby in a rough log cabin "halfway between Claremore and Oologah before there was a town at either place." He rose from a vaudeville career as a sideshow rope-tricks artist to become one of the most popular figures in America, thanks to his folksy humor.

Will Rogers starred on Broadway for 10 years in the *Ziegfield Follies*, wrote an immensely popular national newspaper column, and acted in more than 70 Hollywood movies. Sadly, before he could retire back home to Claremore, Rogers was killed in a plane crash in 1935; his land here was later turned into the **Will Rogers Memorial** (918/341-0719, daily, $5), a mile northwest of downtown Claremore on a hill over-looking the town. A statue of Rogers greets visitors at the front door, and his tomb is here, along with a small archive and museum that recounts his life story, showing off his collections of saddles, lariats, and other cowboy gear.

Another popular Claremore stop is the **J. M. Davis Arms and Historical Museum** (330 N. J.M. Davis Blvd., 918/341-5707, closed Sun. in winter, donations), right off Route 66. Besides housing one of the largest and most comprehensive gun

Will Rogers Memorial

collections anywhere in the world (just under 14,000 firearms!), the museum has antique musical instruments, hundreds of posters dating back to World War I, and 1,200 German beer steins.

For good food and out-of-this-world pies (over a dozen different kinds), stop by the **Hammett House Restaurant** (1616 W. Will Rogers, 918/341-7333), west of downtown next to the Rogers Memorial.

Catoosa: The Blue Whale

One of Tulsa's premier Route 66 attractions was the giant **Blue Whale,** in the suburb of **Catoosa,** northeast of Tulsa along the stretch of the old road that runs from I-44 exit 240. The park, built as an animal-themed tourist attraction in the 1970s by Hugh Davis, a curator at the Tulsa Zoo, closed down long ago and was left to crumble. Unlike so many other long-suffering Route 66 landmarks, however, the Blue Whale has been lovingly restored by the family of its original creators (with a little help from the Hampton Inn brand of Hilton Hotels).

Catoosa, surprisingly, is also a major port, linked, by way of impressively engineered improvements to the Arkansas River system, to the Gulf of Mexico. Even more surprising may be the presence in Catoosa of the 20-story **Hard Rock Casino** (918/266-4352), where there are three acres of gaming, a 24-hour Route 66 Diner, and 450 plush rooms, plus big-name entertainers performing in the state-of-the-art concert hall.

Tulsa

Home to fine art deco buildings built during the 1920s boom years of the Oklahoma oil industry, **Tulsa** (pop. 391,906) is a bustling big city that doesn't make a song-and-dance out of its many treasures. It's a fascinating place to explore. If your time is limited, spend it at one of the country's top art museums, the **Gilcrease Museum** (918/596-2700, closed Mon., $8), on the northwest edge of town. Bought with the fortune benefactor Thomas Gilcrease made when oil was discovered on his land, the collection includes some of the most important works of Western American art and sculpture, with major works by Thomas Moran, George Catlin, and others, plus Native American artifacts and early maps that put the frontier

Tulsa is the home of **Oral Roberts University,** marked by a futuristic, 15-story tower and a 60-foot-high pair of praying hands along Lewis Avenue, six miles south of downtown.

region into its historical context. The expansive grounds include a lovely series of gardens and Mr. Gilcrease's old house.

Due south of downtown Tulsa, the art deco spire of the **Boston Avenue Methodist Church** is a national landmark tower rising over Route 66. South of the Tulsa airport, a few blocks north of Route 66's run along 11th Street, is a different sort of landmark: the **Admiral Twin Drive-In** (7355 E. Easton St., 918/392-9959), which was a key setting in S. E. Hinton's bestselling coming-of-age novel *The Outsiders.*

For dinner or a drink, the liveliest part of Tulsa is the Brookside district, south of downtown around 34th Street and Peoria Avenue, where there's a handful of trendy cafés, nightclubs, and restaurants, including the **R Bar and Grill** (3421 S. Peoria Ave., 918/724-5555). Downtown, you can get a feel for the old days at the retro 1920s **New Atlas Grill** (415 S. Boston Ave., 918/583-3111), serving full breakfasts plus soups, salads, and lunchtime sandwiches in an art deco tower. Much of the old Route 66 frontage along 11th Street near the University of Tulsa has been rediscovered by retro-minded revivalists who enjoy the good honest food at **Tally's Café** (1102 S. Yale Ave., 918/835-8039). Another fixture on Route 66 since the early 1950s is the **El Rancho Grande** (1629 E. 11th St., 918/584-0816), which still offers unreconstructed Mexican food.

The usual chain hotels and motels line all the freeways around Tulsa. There is a big **Holiday Inn** (17 W. 7th St., 918/585-5898, $60 and up) downtown. For the full Route 66 experience, try the renovated and very stylish **Campbell Hotel** (2636 E. 11th St., 855/744-5500, $140 and up).

Old Route 66: Stroud

Between Sapulpa, on the suburban fringes of southwest Tulsa, and the next main stop, Chandler, old Route 66 zigzags back and forth along the freeway for the next 50 miles. Near the east end of this stretch, three miles west of Sapulpa, the circa-1921 **Rock Creek Bridge** is a reminder of what the old roads were really like: 120 feet long yet only 12 feet wide. The truss is rusty but the bridge still stands as a proud reminder of the original 1920s Route 66. Across the bridge is another evocative reminder: an abandoned drive-in movie theater, long closed but with the screen and the fan-shaped parking lot still intact.

Continuing west, old-roads fanatics will probably want to follow the winding alignment of Route 66, which continues along the south side of the turnpike for over 40 miles. On the west side of **Stroud** (pop. 2,690; "Home of Daneka Allen, Miss OK 1999"), check out the **Rock Cafe** (114 W. Main St., 918/968-3990), a Route 66 relic built in 1939 out of local stone quarried when the original highway was cut in the 1920s. The Rock Café (whose bathroom featured original graffiti by *Toy Story* creator John Lasseter, who modeled some scenes in his Route 66 movie *Cars* on the Rock Café's inimitable architecture) suffered from a fire in 2008 but got back up and running in no time and still churns out its better-than-average roadside fare. Stroud also has the classic, old **Skyliner Motel** (717 W. Main St., 918/968-9556, $50 and up).

Chandler and Warwick

West of Stroud, as for most of the way between Tulsa and Oklahoma City, old Route 66 continues along the south side of the I-44 Turnpike, which has another of its very rare exits at **Chandler** (pop. 3,100). Chandler is one of the most pleasant old Route 66 towns in Oklahoma, with a wealth of well-preserved sandstone-and-brick buildings, a trio of which house an enjoyable local history center. It stands out for a number of good reasons, not least of which is the classic **Lincoln Motel** (740 E. 1st St., 405/258-0200, $55), along old Route 66 at the east edge of town. It's a little time-worn, for sure, but still as neat and tidy as the day it opened in 1939 with two dozen two-room cabins, each with a green bench for watching the world whiz by. Chandler's solid-looking WPA-era Armory has been done up to house the lively and engaging **Route 66 Interpretive Center** (400 E. Route 66/1st St., 405/258-1300, closed Sun. in winter and Mon. year-round, $5), which gives an eye-opening introduction to the enterprising and welcoming Route 66 spirit. There's a public swimming pool (summer only), a gallery run by Route 66 artist Jerry McClanahan (903/467-6384, appt. only), and a well-restored cottage-style Phillips 66 station.

Heading west toward Oklahoma City, old Route 66 continues along the south side of I-44, passing a metal-roofed barn emblazoned with a photogenic "Meramec Caverns—Stanton MO" sign

READING UP ON ROUTE 66

Considering the old road's great fame, it's hardly surprising that over a dozen different books in print deal with the Route 66 experience. Some are travel guides, some folk histories, others nostalgic rambles down what was and what's left along the Mother Road. Photographic essays document the rapidly disappearing architecture and signage, and at least one cookbook catalogs recipes of dishes served in cafés on the route. Even in the age of GPS coordinates, online maps, and Twitter feeds (like the timely and accurate Route 66 News), nothing beats a good book. The following is a sampling of favorite titles, most of which can be found in stores along the route if not in your local bookstore.

The Grapes of Wrath, John Steinbeck (Penguin Books). The first and still most compelling Route 66-related story traces the traumatic travels of the Joad family from Dust Bowl Oklahoma to the illusive Promised Land of California. Brutally vivid, *The Grapes of Wrath* was an instant bestseller at the tail end of the Depression and was the source of Route 66's appellation, "The Mother Road."

A Guide Book to Highway 66, Jack Rittenhouse (University of New Mexico Press). A facsimile reprinting of the self-published 1946 book that the late author sold door-to-door at truck stops, motor courts, and cafés along the route.

west of Chandler and crossing under the freeway about three miles west of **Warwick.** From here, one of the state's best surviving stretches of Route 66, known locally as the "free road," runs for over 30 miles along the north side of the turnpike, passing by horse and cattle ranches as it rolls across the red earth.

On old Route 66, about seven miles west of Chandler and a few miles east of where Route 66 again crosses the I-44 Turnpike (at exit 158), the old highway town of Warwick has a small gem: the **Seaba Station Motorcycle Museum** (405/258-9141, closed Wed., free), a simple 1920s filling station, recently and thoughtfully renovated to house a covetable collection of motorcycles, memorabilia, fan magazines, and more. My favorite item is a 1970s Evel Knievel pinball machine. Altogether there are around 60 motorbikes on display, mostly one-of-a-kind racing and motocross machines.

EZ 66: Route 66 Guide for Travelers, Jerry McClanahan (National Historic Route 66 Federation). The most-detailed driver's guide to old Route 66, packed with maps and mile-by-mile instructions and information, spiral-bound for on-the-road ease of use.

Route 66: The Mother Road, Michael Wallis (St. Martin's Press, 1987). This richly illustrated and thoroughly researched guide to the old road is more armchair companion than practical aid, but the book captures the spirit of Route 66, and the writer has been a key promotional force behind the road's preservation and rediscovery. (Wallis also does the voice of the sheriff in *Cars*.)

Route 66 Sightings, Jerry McClanahan, Jim Ross, and Shellee Graham (Ghost Town Press, 2011). By far the best Route 66 photo book, this lush volume captures the Mother Road in all its moods.

Searching for 66, Tom Teague (Samizdat House, 1996). More personal than other titles on Route 66, this poignant book of vignettes, illustrated with the fine pen-and-ink drawings of Route 66 artist Bob Waldmire, describes the author's interactions with the many people along Route 66 who made it what it was. Sadly, both the author and the artist (and almost everyone profiled) have since passed away, making the stories here all the more important and affecting.

Arcadia

About 10 miles east of the I-35 freeway through OKC, the main stop along this idyllic rural cruise is the old highway town of **Arcadia** (pop. 247), which holds a wonderfully restored, very large, red **round barn** (405/396-0824). The ground floor of this much-loved landmark, originally built way back in 1898, is now a mini museum and gift shop, selling some highly collectible, original Route 66 memorabilia.

A half mile west of the round barn, Arcadia's other Route 66 landmark is bright, shiny, and comparatively new: **Pops** (405/928-7677), a gas station and small café fronted by a giant (66-foot-tall) soda pop bottle-shaped sign (not neon, but multicolored, energy-efficient LEDs). Built by Aubrey McClendon, an Oklahoma-born natural gas billionaire, Pops opened in 2007 and sells over 500 different varieties of soda pop (including around 100 brands of root

North of OKC, Route 66 ran through the town of **Edmond,** the place where aviator Wiley Post is buried (he was the pilot killed in the same crash as Will Rogers). Edmond is also notorious for the fact that a disgruntled post office employee killed 14 of his co-workers here in 1986, inspiring the expression "going postal."

Following old Route 66 across Oklahoma City can be confusing, but keep an eye peeled for a bottle-shaped building on Classen Boulevard at 23rd Street.

beer!), as well as the requisite burgers and fuel, plus silky milk shakes. Even if you're not all that hungry or thirsty, the exuberant, bottle-shaped tower, with its rainbow of colors, makes it worth hanging around till nightfall.

Oklahoma City

Now tragically synonymous with the anti-government terrorist bombing carried out by Timothy McVeigh in 1995, **Oklahoma City** (pop. 579,999) has long been one of the primary stops along the Mother Road. In the Bobby Troup song, it was the only place along the route he singled out for praise ("Oklahoma City is mighty pretty"), no doubt thanks to the easy rhyme, though its wealth of "City Beautiful" era avenues and neighborhoods makes it very enjoyable to explore. The city was the biggest boomtown of the 1889 Land Rush, when Oklahoma was opened for white settlement after being set aside "for eternity" as Indian Territory. Between noon and sundown on April 22, over 10,000 people raced here to claim the new lands—many of them having illegally camped out beforehand, earning the nickname "Sooner," which is still applied to the state's college football team.

A second boom took place during the Depression years, when oil was struck. There are still producing wells in the center of the city, including some on the grounds of the state capitol. The collapse of the oil industry in the 1980s hit hard, but the shock of the 1995 bombing seems to have galvanized the city, which has since revitalized itself with a gorgeous new baseball stadium, an exciting NBA basketball team, a concert arena, and canal-side cafés, all collected in the compact, walkable "Bricktown" warehouse district.

Just off old Route 66 across from the capitol, a good first stop is the **Oklahoma History Center** (800 Nazih Zuhdi Dr.,

405/522-0765, closed Sun., $7), which has exhibits tracing the state's growth, with special collections on the Native American presence and on pioneers. There's also a wide-ranging oral history of the Mother Road.

For poignant balance to a nostalgic Route 66 tour, pay your respects to the 168 men, women, and children killed in the April 19, 1995, bombing of the Alfred P. Murrah Federal Building. Between the capitol and Bricktown, the site of the bombing has been preserved as a **memorial park** (open 24 hours, free), landscaped with a shallow pool around which are arrayed a series of 168 sculpted chairs. Each chair represents a person killed in the blast, and the chairs range from very small to full-sized, marking the varying ages of the dead (who included 19 kids from the building's day-care center). An adjacent **museum** (405/609-8855, daily, $12) tells the story of the bombing, its perpetrators, and its victims.

The Triple-A **Oklahoma City Dodgers** (405/218-1000) play at ever-pleasant Chickasaw Bricktown Ballpark, south of downtown near the junction of I-35 and I-40.

Oklahoma City Practicalities

The downtown Bricktown district is home to a lively concentration of restaurants and bars, many lined up along the attractively-landscaped Bricktown Canal. Near the north edge of Bricktown, **Tapwerks Ale House** (121 E. Sheridan Ave., 405/319-9599) has great beers, good food, and frequent live music. Oklahoma City also has more barbecue stands and steakhouses than just about anywhere in the country. On the old Route 66 landmark alignment northwest of downtown, head to **Jack's BBQ** (4418 NW 39th St., 405/605-7790), a traditional cafeteria-style BBQ joint with very good brisket sandwiches, best washed down with a cold drink next door at the Hideaway Club sports bar. Other good OKC BBQ bets include the

The exciting **Oklahoma City Thunder** NBA basketball team (405/208-4800) plays at Chesapeake Energy Arena, on the west side of the railroad tracks from Bricktown.

bigger and more accessible **Iron Starr Urban BBQ** (3700 N. Shartel Ave., 405/524-5925), just off 36th Street; or **Earl's Rib Palace** (216 Johnny Bench Dr., 405/272-9898), with six locations including one right on the Bricktown Canal. For great, non-barbecue food right on old Route 66, go to the popular **Ann's Chicken Fry House** (405/943-8915)—look for the classic Caddies and fake police cars in the parking lot.

Accommodation options in and around OKC are provided by the usual motel chains, plus a very nice **Hampton Inn** (300 E. Sheridan Ave., 405/232-3600, $150 and up) in Bricktown.

El Reno: Hamburger City

Established as Fort El Reno in 1874 as part of U.S. Army efforts to subdue the Cheyenne, **El Reno** (pop. 16,749) later saw duty as a POW camp during World War II, then earned a measure of fame as the site of a motel seen in the offbeat road movie *Rain Man*. (In the movie, the motel was in Amarillo, but the "real" one, called the Big Eight, sat along old Route 66 at the east edge of El Reno.)

West of Oklahoma City, the first real town beyond the OKC suburbs is **Yukon,** hometown of country crooner Garth Brooks and of a giant "Yukon's Best Flour" grain mill, whose huge sign lights up the night sky and draws shutterbugs off the highway.

For hungry road-trippers, especially those fond of all-American burger joints, El Reno offers an abundance of choices. Three great old places stand within a block of each other along old Route 66. The oldest, **Robert's Grill** (300 S. Bickford St., 405/262-1262), has been cooking since 1926 and should be a national model for short-order cooking. A

block to the west is **Sid's Diner** (300 S. Choctaw St., 405/262-7757), which became insanely popular after it was featured on the TV show *Man vs. Food*. Finally, a block to the east is **Johnnie's Grill** (301 S. Rock Island, 405/262-4721, daily), with the biggest menu and most spacious dining room. All three El Reno burger joints are famous for putting fried onions in and on their burgers. On the first weekend in May, El Reno gets together to cook up the "World's Largest Fried Onion Hamburger," a 750-pound behemoth that inspires an all-day festival.

Hydro: Lucille's Roadhouse

There's no clearer contrast between the charms of the old road and the anonymity of the Interstate than tiny **Hydro,** about midway between Oklahoma City and Clinton on the west bank of the Canadian River. A wonderful length of old Route 66 runs along the north side of I-40 exit 89, right past the ancient service station and souvenir stand operated by Lucille Hamons from 1941 until her death in 2000. Though it's just 50 yards from the fast lane of the freeway, visiting Lucille's place to buy a soda or a postcard and have a quick hello with the energetic proprietor was a Route 66 rite of passage. Lucille's inspired the creation of a replica roadhouse on the north side of I-40 in the next town to the west, Weatherford, called **Lucille's Roadhouse** (580/772-8808).

West of Lucille's, a surviving six-mile stretch of old Route 66 pavement follows the lay of the land up and down, offering a better sense of the landscape than does the faster but duller new road, which was completed in 1966.

Oklahoma Route 66 Museum

Clinton

Named for Judge Clinton Irwin and not for former president Bill, **Clinton** (pop. 9,033) started life as a trading post for local Cheyenne Arapahoe people and is now in the spotlight as home of the official **Oklahoma Route 66 Museum** (2229 W. Gary Blvd., 580/323-7866, daily, closed Sun. and Mon. in winter, $5), near the west end of town. Unlike many other "museums" along the route, this one is a true showcase and not just another souvenir

Welcome to Texola!

stand. Funded by a variety of state and local sources, the museum opened in 1995 after undergoing a massive, million-dollar expansion and improvement. Collectors from all over the country, including Clinton's own Gladys Cuthbert, whose husband, Jack Cuthbert, was the primary promoter of Route 66 throughout its glory years, donated signs, artifacts, and memorabilia, which have been organized into a comprehensive exhibition of Mother Road history and culture not to be missed by any Route 66 aficionado. (There's a good gift shop, too.)

Just east of the Texas/Oklahoma border, **Texola** (pop. 36) has dried up and all but blown away since it was bypassed by I-40, but a few remnants still stand, awaiting nostalgic photographers.

Childhood home of country-western star Toby Keith, Clinton also has the very nice **McLain Rogers public park,** with a swimming pool and water slide, at the center of town along 10th Street (old Route 66), next to the Route 66 Miniature Golf Course.

For food, west of town along the I-40 frontage, just north of exit 62, **Jigg's Smoke House** (580/323-5641) is a tiny cabin specializing in travel-friendly beef jerky. The slightly faded **Trade Winds Inn** (2128 W. Gary Blvd., 580/323-2610, $50 and up), across from the Route 66 museum, played host to Elvis Presley at least four times. Elvis's room has been "preserved" as a mini shrine, and you can stay in it (for around $100) and experience a time warp back to the mid-1960s. There's also a Hampton Inn and many other national chains.

Elk City

The last—or first, depending on your direction—sizable town east of the Texas border is **Elk City** (pop. 11,693), "Home of Susan Powell, Miss America 1981," and also childhood home of songwriter Jimmy Webb, who penned such all-time classics as "Galveston," "Wichita Lineman," "MacArthur Park," and "Up, Up and Away." Elk City was a popular stopover on Route 66, as evidenced by the many old motels along the various alignments of the old highway through town. Long before Elk City had its Route 66 heyday, it was a wild frontier town along the cattle trails from Texas to Dodge City, Kansas. The area's cowboy and pioneer history is recounted in the **Old Town Museum** (580/225-6266, daily, $5), on the far west side of town, where there's a re-created Wild West town, complete with doctor's office, schoolhouse, tepee, and rodeo museum. A newer addition to Old Town Museum is the official **National Route 66 Museum,** which has a *huge* Route 66 shield outside; inside there's an old pickup truck decorated to look like the one from *The Grapes of Wrath* and lots of other old-road memorabilia.

During the 1940s, oil and gas were discovered underground in the Anadarko Basin, and the town experienced another short boom, a time remembered by the towering **"Rig 114,"** a record-breaking, 180-foot-tall drilling rig, installed after its retirement in the park next to the **Casa Grande Hotel** (107 E. 3rd St.). Though fossil fuels have had their ups and downs, in recent years the industry has been on the upswing, leading city fathers to proclaim Elk City the "National Gas Capital of the World."

Elk City has one more surefire Route 66 attraction: the delectable French Silk pie (butter, sugar, and vanilla served in a graham cracker crust) baked at the **Country Dove Tea Room** (610 W. 3rd St., 580/225-7028).

Sayre

If you want a quick flashback to the dark days of Steinbeck's *The Grapes of Wrath*, turn north off I-40 into sleepy **Sayre** (pop. 4,375). The landmark **Beckham County Courthouse,** which looms over the east end of Main Street, was prominently featured in the movie version as Henry Fonda and the rest of the Joads rattled down Route 66 toward California. The Depression era also lives on in the cool and pleasant WPA-era swimming pool in **Sayre City Park,** in between the old Route 66 alignments. Just off the old road, take a look in the ever-expanding **Shortgrass Country Museum** (106 E. Poplar Ave., 580/928-5757, Tues.-Fri. 9am-noon, free), housed in the old Rock Island Line railroad depot, with changing displays documenting regional history from Cheyenne times to the arrival of homesteading settlers during the great Land Rush of 1892. East of the museum stands a giant grain elevator that has rusted into a gorgeous orange glow.

Erick

In Jack D. Rittenhouse's original *A Guide Book to Highway 66*, published in 1946 and now widely available in reprinted versions, he described **Erick** (pop. 1,052) as "the first town you encounter, going west, which has any of the true western look, with its wide, sun-

Sandhills Curiosity Shop

baked street, frequent horsemen, occasional sidewalk awnings, and similar touches." His description still rings true today (apart from the horses, which have been replaced by pickup trucks). Along with main streets named for hometown musical heroes Sheb "Flying Purple People Eater" Wooley and Roger "King of the Road" Miller, Erick has another unique draw: All the buildings at the main intersection, and the only stoplight in town, have chamfered corners, filed off to give a sense of consistency and improve the view. One of the original buildings is gone, so it's not perfect, but another has been resuscitated to house the **Roger Miller Museum** (580/526-3833, closed Mon.-Tues.). Established by the widow of the original "King of the Road," it shows off many old photos, posters, and personal items.

Erick is a very quiet but welcoming little town, especially if you walk around the corner from the Miller Museum to the **Sandhills Curiosity Shop** (hours vary, free). Marked by the dozens of old signs hanging outside the old City Meat Market, this old curiosity shop is owned and operated by a husband-and-wife musical duo who call themselves the Mediocre Music Makers and frequently perform for visitors.

A mile south of the I-40 freeway (exit 7), a nice stretch of late-model Route 66 continues west from Erick as a four-lane divided highway, all the way to Texas through the borderline ghost town of Texola.

TEXAS

Known as the Panhandle because of the way it juts
north from the rest of Texas, this part of the route
is a nearly 200-mile stretch of pancake-flat plains.
Almost devoid of trees or other features, the western half, stretching into New Mexico, is also known
as the Llano Estacado or "Staked Plains," possibly because early travelers marked their route by driving stakes
into the earth. The Texas Panhandle was the southern extent of the
buffalo-rich grasslands of the Great Plains, populated by roving bands
of Kiowa and Comanche Indians as recently as 100 years ago. Now oil
and gas production, as well as trucking and Route 66 tourism, have
joined ranching as the region's economic basis.

Even more so than in New Mexico or Oklahoma, old Route 66
has been replaced by I-40 most of the way across Texas, though
in many of the ghostly towns, like **McLean, Shamrock,** or **Vega,**
and the sole city, **Amarillo,** old US-66 survives as the main business strip, lined by the empty remains of roadside businesses. A
select few are still open for a cup of coffee and a sharp taste of
the living past.

McLean

McLean (pop. 778) was founded around the turn of the 20th century
by an English rancher, Alfred Rowe, who later lost his life on the
Titanic in 1912. Considering its minimal size, McLean is now perhaps
the most evocative town along the Texas stretch of Route 66.
Bypassed only in the early 1980s, the old main drag is eerily silent,
with a few businesses—such as a boot shop and a fine Texas-shaped
neon sign—still standing despite the near-total drop in passing trade.

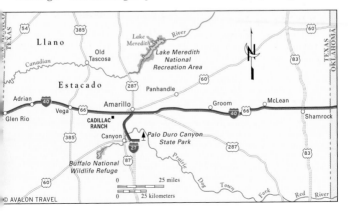

© AVALON TRAVEL

McLean is headquarters of the state's Old Route 66 Association, and efforts are being made to preserve the town in prime condition, which explains the lovingly restored Phillips 66 station at 1st and Gray Streets (on the westbound stretch of old Route 66—the

pumps price gas at 19 cents a gallon!) and the many other odds and ends on display around town. The center of activity here is the wonderful **Devil's Rope Museum** (100 S. Kingsley St., 806/779-2225, closed Sun., closed Dec. 1-Mar. 1, free), at the east end of downtown, which has a huge room full of barbed wire—the "devil's rope"—and some of the most entertaining and educational collections of Route 66 memorabilia you'll find anywhere. No hype, just lots of good stuff and friendly people telling you all about it.

Besides the barbed wire museum, a pair of places next to each other at the west end of McLean offer good food and reliably clean and pleasant rooms: Try the thick steaks, juicy catfish, and weekend barbecue at the **Red River Steak House** (101 W. Route 66, 806/779-8940), then sleep at the **Cactus Inn** (101 Pine St., 806/779-2346).

Groom

The town of **Groom** (pop. 574), 40 miles east of Amarillo on the north side of I-40 at exit 113, holds two of the more eye-catching sights along old Route 66. One of these is a water tower on the north side of I-40 that leans like the Tower of Pisa, causing drivers to stop and rub their eyes, then stop and pull out the camera to take some snapshots to show the folks back home. The other landmark is even harder to miss, a gigantic stainless steel cross—just shy of 200 feet tall and weighing 1.25 tons. This was the largest cross in the western hemisphere until a competitive copycat erected

leaning water tower near Groom

CADILLAC RANCH

No, you're not seeing things—there really are nearly a dozen Cadillacs upended in the Texas plain west of Amarillo, roughly midway between Chicago and Los Angeles. Two hundred yards south of I-40 between the Hope Road and Arnot Road exits (numbers 62 and 60, respectively), some six miles west of Amarillo where old US-66 rejoins the Interstate, the rusting hulks of 10 classic Caddies are buried nose-down in the dirt, their upended tail fins tracing design changes from 1949 to 1964.

A popular shrine to America's love of the open road, **Cadillac Ranch** was created by the San Francisco-based Ant Farm artists' and architects' collective in May 1974, under the patronage of the eccentric Amarillo helium millionaire Stanley Marsh III. The cars were all bought, some running, some not, from local junkyards and used car lots at an average cost of $200 each. Before the Cadillacs were planted in the ground, all the hubcaps and wheels were welded on, a good idea since most of the time the cars are in a badly vandalized state. Tagging the cars with spray-paint graffiti has become a popular activity, but every once in a while advertising agencies and rock bands tidy them up for use as backdrops during photo shoots. In the late 1990s, Cadillac Ranch got another 15 minutes of fame when Marsh decided to dig them up and move them two miles west from where they'd been—to escape the ever-expanding Amarillo sprawl and preserve the nat-

ural horizon. Marsh's death in 2014 have made the site's future less secure, so see it while you can.

There's a well-worn path from the frontage road if you want a closer look. Visitors are allowed any time, day or night.

a slightly taller one along I-70 in Effingham, Illinois. Erected by a religious group in 1995, the Groom cross stands above a series of sculptures depicting biblical scenes and the evils of abortion.

Amarillo

At the heart of the Llano Estacado, midway across the Texas Panhandle, **Amarillo** (pop. 191,000; pronounced "am-uh-RILL-o")

Most of the Texas Panhandle's 20 inches of annual rain falls during summer thunderstorms that sweep across the plains between May and August.

The Great Plains region, and Amarillo in particular, was one of the few places on earth where lighter-than-air helium has been found in an easily recoverable form. An estimated 90 percent of the world's supply once came from here. Today, the Amarillo region is home to the largest wind farms in the USA.

Dynamite Museum consists of a series of surreal street signs placed around Amarillo, that say things like "Road Does Not End," "Lubbock is a Grease Spot," and "Remember You Promised Yourself This Would Be a Good Day."

is a busy, big city that retains its cowboy roots. Center of the local ranching industry that handles some two million head of cattle each year, Amarillo handles nearly 90 percent of all the beef in Texas and some 25 percent of the national total.

Old Route 66 followed 6th Street through Amarillo, past the brick-paved streets of the Old San Jacinto district around Western Avenue, where you can wander amongst ancient-looking gun and saddle shops, numerous Wild West-themed clothing shops, and kitsch-minded antiques shops. To eat and drink with the Coors-drinking cowboys and cowgirls of Amarillo, head west to the **Golden Light Cafe** (2906 SW. 6th Ave., 806/374-9237), a fairly funky roadhouse famed for burgers, homemade hot sauce, green-chile stew, and Frito pies. Next door, the Golden Light Cantina hosts frequent live music. Amarillo is best known for its many good steakhouses, the most famous of which has to be the 450-seat **Big Texan Steak Ranch** (7701 I-40 East, 806/372-6000), which started in 1960 along historic Route 66 and now stands on the east side of Amarillo, off I-40 exit 74, marked by a false-front Wild West town and a giant cowboy atop a billboard. This is the place where they offer a free, 72-ounce steak, provided you eat it all—plus a table full of salad, baked potato, and dessert—in under an hour. If you don't finish everything, the cost is around $72; regular meals and very good "normal" steaks are available as well.

There's a nice motel featuring a Texas-shaped swimming pool at the **Big Texan** (806/372-5000, $70 and up), and dozens of moderate chain motels stand along the I-40 and I-27 frontages, so rooms shouldn't be hard to find.

Palo Duro Canyon State Park

Lovely **Palo Duro Canyon State Park** (daily, $5), one of the most beautiful places in all of Texas, is just 25 miles southeast of

Palo Duro Canyon State Park

Amarillo, east of the town of Canyon off the I-27 freeway. Cut into the Texas plain by the Prairie Dog Town Fork of the Red River, Palo Duro stretches for over 100 miles, with canyon walls climbing to 1,000 feet. Coronado and company were the first Europeans to lay eyes on the area, and numerous Plains tribes, including Apache, Kiowa, and Comanche, later took refuge here. From the end of Hwy-217, a well-paved road winds past the Palo Duro park **visitors center** (806/488-2227, daily), from where a short trail leads to a canyon overlook. Beyond here, the road drops down into the canyon and follows the river on a 15-mile loop trip through the canyon's heart. It's prettiest in spring and fall, and fairly popular year-round.

On your way to or from Palo Duro Canyon, be sure to stop by the excellent **Panhandle-Plains Historical Museum** (2503 4th Ave., 806/651-2244, closed Sun., $10) in the neighboring town of Canyon. One of the state's great museums, this has extensive exhibits on the cultural and economic life of the Panhandle region and its relations with Mexico, the Texas Republic, and the United States. The museum, which is housed in a WPA-era building on the campus of West Texas A&M University, has a special section on rancher Charles Goodnight (1836-1929), who once owned a half million acres here, invented the "chuckwagon," and was an early advocate of saving the bison from extinction.

Vega and Adrian: Midpoint Cafe

Between Amarillo and the New Mexico border, the landscape is made up of endless flat plains dotted with occasional oil derricks and Aermotor windmills. The one biggish town, **Vega** (pop. 884), has a very photogenic collection of former and still-functioning businesses, including the **Boot Hill Saloon and Grill** (806/267-2904), right on Route 66 (Vega Boulevard) at the center of town, and a nicely preserved 1920s Magnolia service station.

West of Vega, the main event hereabouts is both a geographical and culinary magnet: the hamlet of **Adrian** (pop. 166) and the unmissable **Midpoint Cafe** (806/538-6379, daily Apr.-Nov.). One of the route's most enjoyable places to eat, located more or less at the halfway point in Route 66's long ride between Chicago and Los Angeles—both of which are 1,139 miles away—the Midpoint is friendly, has great food, and basically epitomizes all that old-fashioned hospitality that makes Route 66 such a special experience. Be sure to check out the fine selection of Route 66 books and "midpoint" souvenirs, or just stop by for a piece of baked-from-scratch Ugly Crust pie. As more than one satisfied customer has said, you can taste the happiness.

NEW MEXICO

Following old Route 66 across New Mexico gives you a great taste of the Land of Enchantment, as the state calls itself on its license plates. There is less of the actual "old road" here than in other places, but the many towns and ghost towns along I-40, built more or less on top of Route 66, still stand. Route 66 runs around the historic heart of the state's cultural and political capital, **Santa Fe,** and right through the heart of its sprawling Sun Belt commercial center, **Albuquerque.** In other places finding the old road and bypassed towns can take some time, though the effort is usually well rewarded.

Western New Mexico has the most to see and the most interesting topography, with sandstone mesas looming in the foreground and high, pine-forested peaks rising in the distance. Paralleling the Burlington Northern Santa Fe Railway, the route passes through the heart of this region. Numerous detours—to **Inscription Rock** and **Chaco Canyon,** among others—make unforgettable stops along the way. In the east, the land is flatter and the landscape drier as the road transitions from the Great Plains.

Tucumcari

Subject of one of the most successful advertising campaigns in Route 66's long history of roadside hype, **Tucumcari**

The border between Texas and New Mexico marks the boundary between central and mountain time zones. Set your clocks and watches accordingly.

(pop. 5,363) looks and sounds like a much bigger place than it is. Also known as "the town that's two blocks wide and two miles long" (though Tucumcari Boulevard, which follows the route blazed by old Route 66 through town, stretches for closer to seven miles between Interstate exits), Tucumcari does have a little of everything, including a great range of neon signs, but it can be hard to explain the attraction of the town that hundreds of signs along the highways once trumpeted as Tucumcari Tonite—2,000 Motel Rooms. (A new ad campaign plays on this legacy, but signs now say Tucumcari Tonite—1,200 Motel Rooms.)

Hype or no hype, Tucumcari is a handy place to break a journey, and even if you think you can make it to the next town, you will never regret stopping here for a night. Especially if you stop at the famous **Blue Swallow Motel** (815 E. Route 66, 575/461-9849, $70 and up), which no less an authority than *Smithsonian* magazine called "the last, best, and friendliest of the old-time motels." Thanks to the warm hospitality of longtime owner Lillian Redman, few who stayed there during her long reign would disagree, and more recent owners have kept up the old spirit while improving the plumbing and replacing the mattresses. Each room comes with its own garage, and the neon sign alone is worth staying awake for. If the Blue Swallow is full, as it often is, try one of Tucumcari's other old-fashioned motels: the **Motel Safari** (722 E. Route 66, 575/461-1048, $55 and up), a block away, has Wi-Fi and flat-screen TVs, while the **Historic Route 66 Motel** (1620 E. Route 66, 575/461-1212, $40 and up) is clean and stylish, with a Rat Pack-era Palm Springs vibe and Tucumcari's best espresso bar. (Admittedly, it is Tucumcari's *only* espresso bar, but it is nonetheless appreciated.)

Across Route 66 from the Blue Swallow stands another survivor, the landmark tepee fronting the historic **Tee**

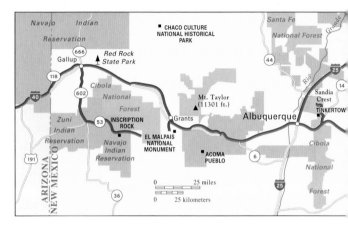

Pee Curios (924 E. Route 66, 575/461-3773), where friendly own-
ers Mike and Betty Callens will tempt you to add to your collection of Southwest or Route 66 souvenirs (or "Damn Fine Stuff," as
their business cards have it). The Tee Pee has one of the coolest
neon signs anywhere, so time your visit to see it in its full glory.

To enjoy the Mexican food as well as a photo opportunity, head
to **La Cita** (575/461-7866), under the turquoise, yellow, and brown
sombrero on the corner of 1st Street and old Route 66. A few
blocks east is the popular **Del's Restaurant** (1202 E. Route 66,
575/461-1740). Three blocks north of Route 66, next to Tucumcari
Ranch and Farm Supply is **Watson's Bar-B-Que** (502 S. Lake St.,
575/461-9620), a trailer-and-picnic-tables place. It's worth the
60-second detour for the smoky but juicy beef brisket, pinto beans,
and green chile stew.

Three newer additions fill out Tucumcari's roster of attractions:
one is a chromed steel **Route 66 sculpture,** welcoming travelers at
the west edge of town; another is the vivid Route 66 mural painted
on the corner of 2nd Street. The third is the unique **Mesalands
Dinosaur Museum** (222 E. Laughlin St., 575/461-3466, closed Sun.
and Mon., $6.50), two blocks north of Route 66. Housed inside
Mesa Community College, the museum boasts "the largest collection of life-sized bronze prehistoric skeletons in the world," plus
real fossils, unusual minerals, and a full-size skeleton of the rare
Torvosaurus, a cousin of legendary *Tyrannosaurus rex*.

Santa Rosa

The I-40 freeway has bisected the town of **Santa Rosa** (pop. 2,750)
and cut its old Route 66 frontage in two, but for over 65 years, trav-

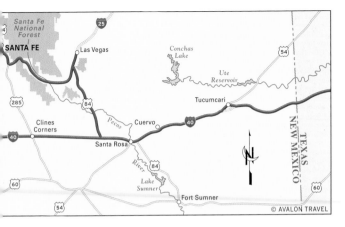

elers crossing New Mexico along Route 66 and I-40 made a point of stopping here for a meal at Club Cafe, "The Original Route 66 Restaurant Since 1935." Thanks to signs lining the road for miles in both directions, emblazoned with the smiling face of the "Fat Man," the Club Cafe was nationally famous for its always-fresh food until it closed in 1992.

Just off the freeway, east of downtown on Route 66 and marked by a hard-to-miss bright yellow hot rod perched atop a 30-foot pole, the **Route 66 Auto Museum** (2866 Historic Route 66, 575/472-1966, $5) has a wide-ranging exhibit on "anything to do with wheels," highlighted by some tricked-out old Fords and Chevys and a totally cherry 1957 T-Bird convertible.

Santa Rosa's other main attraction is unique: the **Blue Hole,** an 80-foot-wide, 80-foot-deep artesian well filled with water so crystal-clear that it draws scuba divers from all over the western states to practice their underwater techniques here. The water of the Blue Hole, at around 61°F, is too cold for casual swimming, but in the summer heat it's a great place to cool your heels. The Blue Hole is

scuba diver in the Blue Hole

well signed at the end of Blue Hole Road, a half mile south of old Route 66; for purists, Blue Hole Road is *old, old* Route 66, since it formed the early (pre-1937) alignment of the Mother Road across Santa Rosa, the rest of which is used as a runway at the city's airport (no cars allowed!). East of

BUDDY HOLLY, CLOVIS MAN

South of Tucumcari, at the edge of the desolate Llano Estacado that stretches south and east across the Texas Panhandle, the city of Clovis is a large railroad and ranching town that has two unique claims to fame. It is the site where some of the oldest archaeological remains ever found in North America were unearthed: In the 1930s, archaeologists dug up bones and arrowheads that proved human habitation dating back as early as 9000 BC. Some of these artifacts, belonging to what archaeologists have dubbed "Clovis Man," are on display at the **Blackwater Draw Museum** (575/562-2202, daily, $3), on US-70 about 20 miles south of Clovis.

Clovis also played a part in early rock 'n' roll: Buddy Holly came here from Lubbock, across the Texas border, in the late 1950s to record "Peggy Sue," "That'll Be The Day," and other

early classics. You can tour the restored **Norman Petty Recording Studios** (1313 W. 7th St., 575/763-3435), open only by appointment. Buddy's contributions to western culture are also well documented in his hometown of **Lubbock.**

here, running along the south side of I-40, one of the oldest stretches of Route 66 is only partly paved and best done in a 4WD or on a mountain bike. Here you get an indelible sense of what travel was like in the very early days, when less than half of the route's 2,400-odd miles were paved.

Tinkertown and the Sandia Crest

Not that there's any shortage of wacky roadside Americana along what's left of Route 66, but one of the most endearing of them all, **Tinkertown Museum** (505/281-5233, daily Apr.-Oct., $3.50), is a quick 10-minute drive north of the old road. Like an old-fashioned penny arcade run riot, Tinkertown is a marvelous assembly of over a thousand delicately carved miniature wooden figures, arranged in tiny stage sets to act out animated scenes—a circus Big Top complete with side show, a Wild West town with dance-hall girls

Tinkertown

and a squawking vulture—all housed in a ramshackle building made in part out of glass bottles and bicycle wheels, created over the past 50-odd years by Ross and Carla Ward and family. It's impossible to describe the many odds and ends on show here—one display case holds over 100 plastic figures taken from the tops of wedding cakes, for example—especially since the whole thing is always being improved and "tinkered" with. The spirit of the place is aptly summed up in the Tinkertown motto: "We Did All This While You Were Watching TV." The Dalai Lama loved it, and so will you.

To get to Tinkertown, turn off I-40 at exit 175, six miles east of Albuquerque, and follow Hwy-14 for six miles, toward Sandia Crest. Tinker-town is on Hwy-536, 1.5 miles west of the Hwy-14 junction, hidden off the highway among the juniper trees.

Sandia Crest itself is another 12 miles uphill at the end of Hwy-536 National Scenic Byway; the ridge offers a phenomenal panorama from an elevation of 10,678 feet.

Albuquerque

Roughly located at the center of New Mexico, the sprawling city of **Albuquerque** (pop. 545,852) spreads along the banks of the Rio Grande and east to the foothills of 10,000-foot Sandia Crest. By far the state's biggest city, Albuquerque is a young, energetic, and vibrantly multicultural community, which, among many features, boasts a great stretch of old Route 66 along Central Avenue through the heart of the

Along the Pecos River via US-84, some 50 miles southeast of Santa Rosa, the gravesite of Wild West legend Billy the Kid lies just steps from the **Old Fort Sumner Museum** (575/355-2942, $5) in Fort Sumner, where 7,000 Navajo people were imprisoned from 1864 to 1869. A visit to the grave is free. To learn more about the Kid, stop by the private museum about three miles from downtown Fort Sumner.

Clines Corners, midway between Albuquerque and Santa Rosa off I-40 exit 218, is a truck stop café that dates back to 1934 and is, as the signs say, Worth Waiting For—for the huge gift shop and the "Cleanest Restrooms on I-40."

Though most people associate computer giant Microsoft with Seattle, the company actually began here in Albuquerque in 1975, in a series of dingy Route 66 motels.

Albuquerque was also the home of the great travel writer and World War II war correspondent Ernie Pyle. His old house at 900 Girard Avenue, a half mile north of Central Avenue, is now the city's oldest public library, which includes his collected works and a few personal items in a small display.

city—18 miles of diners, motels, and sparkling neon signs.

One of the best parts of town is **Old Town,** the historic heart of Albuquerque. Located a block north of Central Avenue, at the west end of Route 66's cruise through downtown, Old Town offers a quick taste of New Mexico's Spanish colonial past, with a lovely old church, the 300-year-old **San Felipe de Neri,** as well as shops and restaurants set around a leafy green park. An information booth in the park has maps of Old Town and other information about the city. Another Old Town attraction, one that carries on the Route 66 tradition of reptile farms and private zoos, is the **American International Rattlesnake Museum** (202 San Felipe St., 505/242-6569, daily, $5), southeast of the main square, where you can see a range of rattlers from tiny babies to full-sized diamondbacks, about 50 all together, plus fellow desert-dwellers like tarantulas and a giant Gila monster.

A very different look into New Mexico's varied cultural makeup is offered at the **Indian Pueblo Cultural Center** (2401 12th St., 505/843-7270, daily, $6), a block north of I-40 exit 158. The center is owned and operated by the state's 19 different Pueblo communities. Its highlight is a fine museum tracing the history of the region's Native American cultures, from Anasazi times up to the Pueblo Revolt of 1680, with the contemporary era illustrated by video presentations and a mock-up of a typical tourist—camera, shorts, and all. On most weekends ceremonial dances are held in the central courtyard—$6 and open to the general public. There's also a small cafeteria where you can sample food like fry bread and atole, and a smoke shop selling discount cigarettes.

Downtown Albuquerque has been under reconstruction seemingly forever, with an ambitious mixed-use project surrounding the train station and massive old Santa Fe Railroad yards. Despite budget shortfalls, the state has pledged money for it, so someday the area may feature the enticingly named **Wheels Museum** (1501 SW 1st St., 505/243-6269), tracing (surprise, surprise . . .) transportation in New Mexico.

Albuquerque Practicalities

The largest city in New Mexico, Albuquerque makes a very handy point of entry for tours of the southwestern United States. For old-road fans, the best stretch of Route 66 through Albuquerque is probably the section along Nob Hill, east of downtown near the University of New Mexico. Here you'll find vintage neon and some great places to eat and drink, including **Kelly's Brew Pub** (3222 E. Central Ave., 505/262-2739), housed in a 1930s Streamline Moderne auto dealership, and the upscale **Monte Vista Fire Station** (3201 E. Central Ave., 505/255-2424). For a taste of 1950s Americana (and good root beer), head to the **Route 66 Malt Shop** (3800 E. Central Ave., 505/242-7866), originally housed in an old gas station and motor court but now occupying a new purpose-built home.

Between Nob Hill and downtown, the excellent **66 Diner** (1405 NE Central Ave., 505/247-1421) serves top-quality burgers and shakes, and regional specialties like green chile chicken. Perhaps the best breakfasts are at the super stylish **Grove Cafe & Market** (600 E. Central Ave., 505/248-9800) in downtown's Huning-Highland Historic District.

New Mexico's long relationship with radioactivity is reflected in the name of Albuquerque's very popular Colorado Rockies-affiliated Triple-A baseball club, the **Isotopes** (505/924-2255, $15 and up), who play just south of downtown. Games are broadcast on **KNML 610 AM.**

Another good range of places to eat lies within walking distance of Old Town, close to the Rio Grande. Enjoy a delicious mix of Mexican and American diner food at **Garcia's Kitchen** (1736 SW Central Ave., 505/842-0273), beneath a glorious neon sign. Fans of the TV show *Breaking Bad* may want to pay their respects to Walt and Jesse at the **Dog House Drive In** (1216 W. Central Ave., 505/243-1019), whose blinking neon sign appeared in a number of episodes. Another old Route 66 landmark, **Mac's La Sierra** (6217 NW Central Ave., 505/836-1212), serves up steak fingers and other beefy specialties in a cozy, dark wood dining room a long ways west of town.

Santa Fe

An hour away from Albuquerque via I-25 or its old road equivalents, Santa Fe (pop. 67,947) is one of the prime vacation destinations in the country. New Mexico's state capital has been at the center of Southwest life for centuries, and the cultural crossroads of a region that has been settled for thousands of years. From the east, detour north from Clines Corners via US-285, or for the full "Historic Route 66" tour follow US-84 north near Santa Rosa toward Las Vegas (the original one, here in New Mexico), then continue west on I-25, parallel to the pioneer-era Santa Fe Trail.

Despite its swirling hordes of vacationers, and its vast infrastructure of hotels, restaurants, art galleries, and souvenir shops, Santa Fe remains one of the most enjoyably un-American small cities. It makes the most sense to begin your tour of Santa Fe at its center, the **Plaza.** This will help you get not only your geographical bearings but also a historical context with which to appreciate the rest of Santa Fe. On the north side of the Plaza, the **Palace of the Governors** (105 W. Palace Ave., closed Mon., $9) is the oldest continuously used public building in America. Dating from 1610, the palace served as residence for Spanish, Mexican, and, later, American territorial governors until 1909, when the New Mexico legislature voted to turn the building into the Museum of New Mexico. The museum contains an excellent overview of the building's and the city's tumultuous history, numerous artifacts and documents, and an exhaustive collection of regional photographs.

To get a sense of the life and work of the woman who did as much as anyone to fix Santa Fe in the American mind, walk two blocks west and one block north from the Plaza to the **Georgia O'Keeffe Museum** (217 Johnson St., 505/946-1000, daily, $12), which contains 1,149 pieces of the late artist's work. Many of the paintings here depict the landscape in and around her home at Abiquiu, north of Santa Fe, where she lived for 40 years.

Shops, shops, and more shops (plus a few cafés and restaurants) line the streets emanating from the Plaza. Many of these have a decidedly upscale bent; there are about 200 art galleries alone in Santa Fe, for

instance (though the most engaging and scenic stretch of them is found along narrow and tree-lined Canyon Road, which runs east from Paseo de Peralta up into the foothills above town). Once you penetrate Santa Fe's Paseo de Peralta, the historic ring road encircling the 17th-century city center, leave your car at one of the many parking lots or garages and see Santa Fe on foot. Another downtown street, Old Pecos Trail, carried Route 66 for its first dozen years before Santa Fe was bypassed in favor of Albuquerque in 1937.

If you're interested in classical music, the **Santa Fe Chamber Music Festival** (505/983-2075 or 888/221-9836) performances take place in July and August in a variety of atmospheric old Santa Fe buildings.

PRACTICALITIES

It's a pleasant surprise that only moderately deep pockets are needed to find good food or memorable accommodations in Santa Fe. With recipes that show the influence of more than 2,000 years of Native American culture (which contributed three major staples: beans, corn, and squash), some 400 years of Catholic inclusion (chiles, cilantro, cumin, onions, garlic, wheat, rice, and both beef and pork), and a liberal dash of American inventiveness, Santa Fe restaurants serve the world's oldest, newest, and, some say, tastiest cuisines—often all side by side on the very same plates. Menu offerings include dishes like a buttermilk corn cake with smoky chipotle-chile shrimp (and a side of red chile onion rings), *chiles rellenos* stuffed with roast duck and black bean mole sauce, or blue corn turkey enchiladas. Santa Fe's fine food is at least as much a draw as its rich history and magical mountain light.

To ease your way into Santa Fe food, start on the Plaza at the **Plaza Café** (54 Lincoln Ave., 505/982-1664), which has been serving

(continued on next page)

(continued)

no-nonsense meals since it opened in 1918. Part of the fun here is the constant clatter of dishes and silverware, the old-fashioned tile floor, and a rear wall with a giant map of the Southwest. If you don't have time for a full meal (the green chile meatloaf is a specialty), pop in for a helping of Frito pie, which is quite the local delicacy (although the recipe allegedly originated in Texas in the 1930s, when Daisy Doolin, the mother of the Dallas-based founder of Frito-Lay, poured chili over her Fritos and found that she liked it).

Just off the Plaza, and well worth a visit for its addictive breakfast quesadilla (with scrambled eggs, applewood-smoked bacon, Jack cheese, and guacamole), is **Cafe Pasqual's** (121 Don Gaspar Ave., 505/983-9340), which has deliciously inventive dishes at lunch and dinner, too. After a meal elsewhere (unless someone else is paying your expenses!), join Santa Fe's old guard at the **Pink Adobe** (406 Old Santa

Fe Trail, 505/983-7712 or 505/982-9762), also known as simply "The Pink," a very deluxe, retro-minded supper club that's also home to the kitschy Dragon Room bar, a popular late-night hangout.

For a convenient and memorable place to stay, a pair of small B&B gems are within a short walk of the Plaza. **Adobe Abode** (202 Chapelle St., 505/983-3133, $150 and up), as the name suggests, consists of several large adobe-style rooms and casitas, and the **Casa del Toro** (229 McKenzie St., 866/476-1091, $125 and up) has modern baths, upscale amenities, and eclectic antiques and folk furnishings.

If you prefer to park within sight of your room, there's a nice motor inn with a location that's hard to beat: **Garrett's Desert Inn** (311 Old Santa Fe Trail, 505/982-1851 or 800/888-2145, $95 and up), a few blocks off the Plaza. If all the desirable places are full, or if you're tight on funds, cruise along busy Cerrillos Road (Hwy-14), where you'll find all the major chains.

San Felipe de Neri church in
Old Town, Albuquerque

Like most of New Mexico, Albuquerque has a ton of inexpensive accommodations, with all the usual chain motels represented near the airport and along the Interstate frontage roads, plus a lot of fading or extinguished old stars of the Route 66 era, like the famous **El Vado** (2500 W. Central Ave.), which has been in redevelopment limbo for decades. Recently purchased by the city of Albuquerque, the El Vado likely will be redeveloped, perhaps as a public park or farmers market. For a place with oodles of Route 66 character, stay at the neat and tidy, Del Webb-built **Hiway House Motel** (3200 SE Central Ave., 505/268-3971, $55 and up), in the Nob Hill district, or the unimaginatively but accurately named **Monterey Non-Smokers Motel** (2402 SW Central Ave., 505/243-3554, around $70), near Old Town. The nicest hotel has got to be the grand old **Hotel Andaluz** (125 2nd St., 505/242-9090 or 877/987-9090, $160 and up), a block off old Route 66 in the heart of the lively downtown nightlife district. One of the first inns built by New Mexico-born hotel magnate Conrad Hilton, the Andaluz has been thoughtfully and completely restored and updated, and is now the most comfortable and gracious place to stay, with an entrancing rooftop bar offering grand sunset vistas.

Old Route 66: Bernalillo

True fans of the full Route 66 tour, and anyone interested in the art and architecture (and food!) of the American Southwest, will want to make the trip to the state capital, Santa Fe. The original Route 66 alignment ran north from Albuquerque along the I-25 corridor through Las Vegas, then curved back south from Santa Fe along what's now US-84, to rejoin I-40 west of Santa Rosa.

The best sense of this old route across old New Mexico comes just north of Albuquerque, at the historic town of **Bernalillo.** Route 66 here follows the much older El Camino Real, which linked these

Spanish colonies 400 years ago. The heart of Bernalillo contains two great stops, poles apart from each other in ambience but together capturing the essence of the place. First of these is ancient-feeling **Silva's Saloon** (955 Camino del Pueblo, 505/867-9976), whose walls, coated in layers of newspaper clippings, old snapshots, and other mementos, form a fabulously funky backdrop for a cold beer alongside cowboys, bikers, and other characters. Up the street is the stylish **Range Cafe** (925 S. Camino del Pueblo, 505/867-1700), where a spacious dining room has very good "New New Mexican" food (try the bread pudding!) and a sophisticated, big-city air.

Rio Puerco and the Route 66 Casino

Between Albuquerque and Acoma Pueblo, a fine old stretch of old Route 66 survives, passing crumbling tourist courts and service stations across the Laguna Indian Reservation. The photogenic Route 66 highlight here is the graceful old steel truss **Rio Puerco Bridge,** which spans a usually dry river, right alongside the I-40 superslab about 10 miles west of Albuquerque. The old road ambience is also overwhelmed by the huge new **Route 66 Casino,** south of the freeway, the largest of many gambling complexes that have sprung up on Indian reservations across this part of New Mexico. Besides the jinglingly huge, 50,000-square-foot casino (which has the usual card tables, craps, and roulette), the complex also has a 2,800-seat theater, a roadside café, a smoke shop offering cheap (tax-free) tobacco, and a large hotel (866/711-7829, $100 and up).

The heart of the historic Laguna Pueblo, where some 500 people live in adobe buildings around a church that dates from 1699, is not really open to travelers, but just west of the pueblo the old Route 66 frontage runs past an old road landmark: **Budville,** where the remnants of an old trading post and café still stand in atmospheric silence along the south side of the highway.

Acoma Pueblo: Sky City

A dozen miles east of Grants and 50 miles west of Albuquerque, one of the Southwest's most intriguing sites, **Acoma Pueblo,** stands atop a 350-foot-high sandstone mesa. Long known as "Sky City," Acoma is one of the very oldest communities in North America, inhabited since AD 1150. The views out across the plains are unforgettable, especially toward Enchanted Mesa on the horizon to the northeast.

Few people live on the mesa today, though the many adobe houses are used by Pueblo craftspeople, who live down below but come up to the mesa-top to sell their pottery and other crafts to

Acoma Pueblo

tourists. To visit this amazing place, you have to join a guided **tour** (800/747-0181, daily Mar.-Nov., Fri.-Sun. in winter, $23), which begins with a bus ride to the mesa-top and ends with a visit to **San Esteban del Rey Mission,** the largest Spanish colonial church in the state. Built in 1629, the church features a roof constructed of huge timbers that were carried from the top of Mt. Taylor on the backs of neophyte Indians—a distance of more than 30 miles.

Acoma Pueblo is 15 miles south of I-40, from exit 108 (westbound) or exit 96 (eastbound). Start your visit by appreciating the artifacts displayed in the beautiful **Haak'u Museum,** at the base of the mesa, where tours of the ancient Sky City begin. The Acoma tribe also operates the money-spinning **Sky City Casino and Hotel** (888/759-2489, $99 and up), sited well away from the historic core of the pueblo, right off I-40 exit 102.

US-60: Pie Town and the Lightning Field

A long way south of Grants, an old mining camp was so famous for fine desserts it became known as **Pie Town.** After many years of pielessness, local meringue-lovers lucked out when baker Kathy Knapp opened the **Pie-O-Neer Cafe** (575/772-2711, closed Mon.-Wed.), on old US-60 at milepost 59.

East of Pie Town off US-60, more than 20 miles outside Quemado (the next "town" to the west), the **Lightning Field** (505/898-3335,

Acoma Pueblo, or "Sky City"

May-Oct.) is an outdoor "land art" installation by the late great Walter De Maria, who implanted a grid of steel tubes into the high-elevation (7,200 feet above sea level) New Mexico plain with the intention of attracting lightning strikes. The sculpture consists of 400 stainless steel poles, ranging in height from 16 to 27 feet, placed 200 feet apart in a rectangular grid that is roughly one mile by one kilometer. The engineering feat here was to set the poles so that their tops form an exactly level plane. Despite the name, the experience is meant to be about contemplation, rather than spectacle; casual visitors are not allowed, and for the full Lightning Field experience you have to stay overnight in a nearby cabin, and meals and transportation to the site are included in the $150-250 per person fees. The Lightning Field is maintained by the same foundation that curates the intriguing Dia-Beacon museum, north of New York City.

Grants

Along with the usual Route 66 range of funky motels and rusty neon signs, the former mining boomtown of **Grants** (pop. 9,182) has the unique attraction of the **New Mexico Mining Museum** (505/287-4802 or 800/748-2142, closed Sun., $3), right downtown on old Route

New Mexico Mining Museum

66 (Santa Fe Avenue) at the corner of Iron Avenue. Most of the exhibits trace the short history of local uranium mining, which began in 1950 when a local Navajo rancher, Paddy Martinez, discovered an odd yellow rock that turned out to be high-grade uranium ore. Mines around Grants once produced half the ore mined in the United States, but production has ceased (pending renewed interest in nuclear power). From the main gallery, ride the elevator down (only one floor, but it feels like 900 feet) to the highlight of the mining museum: a credible re-creation of a uranium mine, complete with an underground lunch room emblazoned with all manner of warning signs.

The landmark Uranium Café, with its atomic neon sign across Route 66 from the mining museum, has been going in and out of business for years. The latest contestant, **Badlands Burgers** (519 W. Santa Fe Ave., 505/287-5557), has earned a nationwide reputation for classic roadside grub—and a New Mexico State Fair Gold Medal for its green chile cheeseburgers!

Inscription Rock and El Malpais: Hwy-53

Western New Mexico is among the most beautiful places on the planet. South of I-40 and Route 66, one of the best drives through it, Hwy-53, loops between Gallup and Grants across the Zuni and Navajo Nation Indian Reservations. Hwy-53 skirts the southern foothills of the 9,000-foot Zuni Mountains, along the edge of the massive **El Malpais** lava flow—thousands of acres of pitch-black, concrete-hard, glassy, sharp rock sliced and diced by lava tubes and collapsing craters. Formed between 10,000 and 115,000 years ago, most of the Malpais is wild and undeveloped, but on the slopes of Bandera Volcano, you can tour the privately run **Ice Cave** (888/423-2283, daily, closed Nov.-Feb., $12), where the cool temperatures are very welcome on a hot summer's day.

West from El Malpais, the route follows ancient Indian trails that Coronado used on his ill-fated 1540 explorations, winding past piñon-covered hills, open grasslands, and the fascinating graffiti collection of **El Morro National Monument.** Better known as **Inscription Rock,** the 200-foot-high sandstone cliffs of El Morro have been inscribed by travelers like Juan de Oñate, who wrote his name with a flourish in 1605, after he "discovered" the Gulf of California.

Atop the cliffs are the partially excavated remains of a small pueblo dating from around AD 1200. A two-mile loop trail to the inscriptions and the ruins starts from a small **visitors center** (505/783-4226, daily, free), where exhibits outline the history of the site. The trails are closed an hour before sunset, so get here early enough in the day to enjoy the beautiful scenery. There is also a small campground (no showers, pit toilets) amidst the junipers.

Southwest of Inscription Rock, animal lovers may want to visit the **Wild Spirit Wolf Sanctuary** (505/775-3304, closed Mon., $7), where over three dozen wolves and wolf-dogs live on a 100-year-old moonshiner's ranch.

Midway between Grants and Gallup, I-40 crosses the 7,250-foot Continental Divide, where the Top O' the World dance hall used to tempt travelers off old Route 66. From here (exit 47), it's possible to follow the old road for 30 miles, running east along I-40 as far as Grants.

Gallup

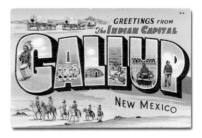

Though it's not exactly scenic, **Gallup** (pop. 20,209) is a fascinating place. Founded in 1881 when the Santa Fe Railroad first rumbled through, and calling itself "The Gateway to Indian Country" because it's the largest town near the huge Navajo and other Native American reservations of the Four Corners region, Gallup has some of the Southwest's largest trading posts and one of the best strips of neon signs you'll see anywhere on old Route 66.

For travelers intent on experiencing a little of the charms of old Route 66, Gallup also has **El Rancho** (1000 E. Route 66, 505/863-9311, $115 and up), a delightful old hotel lovingly preserved in its 1930s glory. Built by a brother of movie director D. W. Griffiths, El Rancho feels like a national park lodge, with a large but welcoming lobby dominated by a huge stone fireplace. All the rooms in the old wing are named for the movie stars who have stayed here over the years—the W. C. Fields Room, the John Wayne Room, the Marx Brothers Room (which sleeps six), even the Ronald Reagan Room—and signed glossies of these and many more actors and actresses adorn the halls. El Rancho also has a good restaurant serving regional food, and a gift shop selling souvenirs and locally crafted jewelry, pottery, and rugs.

Gallup hosts the annual **Inter-Tribal Ceremonial** (505/863-3896), perhaps the largest Native American gathering in the country, held early in August at **Red Rock State Park,** seven miles east of Gallup, and culminating in a parade that brings some 30,000 people out to line old Route 66 through town. Festivities include a rodeo, powwows, and a beauty show.

In the heart of historic downtown, the old Santa Fe train depot (still in use by Amtrak), houses the **Gallup Cultural Center** (201 E. Route 66, 505/863-4131). Free dance shows are staged at the nearby courthouse square nightly

Much less developed, but every bit as memorable as the cliff dwellings of Mesa Verde, the extensive archaeological remains protected inside **Chaco Culture National Historical Park** are well worth your time. Though it's a two-hour drive from I-40 via unpaved roads, the park is one of the wonders of the Southwest desert.

in summer, next to a statue of a World War II Navajo Code Talker. Another place worth spending some time is **Richardson's Cash Pawn and Trading Post** (222 W. Route 66, 505/722-4762). Family-run since 1913, this busy but friendly space is crammed to the rafters with arts, crafts, and pawned goods—Navajo rugs and jewelry, ornately tooled leather saddles, pearl-inlaid guitars, and more—that give a better sense of local lifestyles (and all their ups and downs) than any museum ever could.

If you like huevos rancheros, breakfast burritos, or even diner stand-bys like French toast, you can sample some of the best at the unpretentious but excellent **Plaza Café** (1501 W. Route 66, 505/722-6240), which is way better than it looks amidst the neighboring gas stations and car repair shops.

ARIZONA

If you're not yet a die-hard Route 66 fan, traveling the old route across Arizona is bound to convert you. The high-speed I-40 freeway gives quick access to some of the best surviving stretches of the old road, and these are some of the most captivating parts of Route 66 anywhere. Between the red-rock mesas of New Mexico and the arid desert along the Colorado River, the route runs past dozens of remarkable old highway towns along some of the oldest and longest still-driveable stretches of the Mother Road.

East of **Flagstaff,** the old road is effectively submerged beneath the freeway, which drops down to cross desolate desert, passing through desiccated towns and **Petrified Forest National Park.** Remnants of numerous old roadside attractions—Indian trading posts, wild animal menageries, and **Holbrook**'s famous "Sleep in a Teepee" Wigwam Village—all survive in varying degrees of preservation along Arizona's section of Route 66.

Midway across the state, the route climbs onto the forested (and often snowy) Kaibab Plateau for a look at the mighty **Grand Canyon,** one of the true wonders of the natural world.

Painted Desert and Petrified Forest National Park

Right along the New Mexico border, Arizona welcomes westbound travelers with an overwhelming display of trading-post tackiness—huge concrete tepees stand at the foot of brilliant red-rock mesas,

while gift shops hawk their souvenirs to passing travelers. The gift shops themselves may not be all that attractive, but the old Route 66 frontage road along here, a.k.a. Hwy-118 between exit 8 in New Mexico and exit 357 in Arizona, is truly spectacular, running at the foot of red-rock cliffs. If you like rocks, gems, and petrified wood, a fine collection is for sale at the endearingly strange **Stewart's Petrified Wood Trading Post,** marked by a family of animated dinosaurs at I-40 exit 303.

Petrified Forest National Park

A great introduction to the Four Corners region, the **Hubbell Trading Post National Historic Site** (928/755-3254, $2), 38 miles north of I-40 from exit 333 and a mile west of the town of Ganado, is a frontier store preserved as it was in the 1870s, when trader John Hubbell began buying the beautiful rugs made by local Navajo weavers.

The easternmost 60-mile stretch of I-40 across Arizona is little more than one long speedway, since almost any sign of the old road has been lost beneath the four-lane Interstate. One place that's worth a stop here is **Petrified Forest National Park** (928/524-6228, daily dawn-dusk, $10 per car). The polished petrified wood on display in the visitors center is gorgeous to look at,

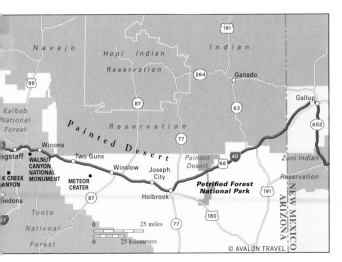

purple sands in the Painted Desert

but seeing 93,000 acres of the stuff in its raw natural state is not, to be honest, particularly thrilling. The story of how the wood got petrified is interesting, though: About 225 million years ago, a forest was buried in volcanic ash, then slowly embalmed with silica and effectively turned to stone. Alongside the visitors center at the entrance to the park, there's a handy restaurant and a gas station.

While the park contains a vast array of prehistoric fossils and pictographs as well as the petrified wood, one of the more interesting sights is the old **Painted Desert Inn,** a Route 66 landmark during the 1920s and 1930s that was converted into a museum and

In and around Holbrook, you'll come across a series of concrete dinosaurs rescued from the old International Petrified Forest Dinosaur Park, which used to stand along I-40 near exit 289.

bookstore after the Park Service took it over in the 1960s. The pueblo-style building, now restored to its 1920s splendor with lovely murals, Navajo rugs and sand paintings, and handcrafted furnishings, is perched on a plateau overlooking the spectacularly colored **Painted Desert** that stretches off toward the northern horizon.

Holbrook: Wigwam Village

Holding a concentrated dose of old Route 66 character, **Holbrook** (pop. 5,100) is definitely worth a quick detour off the I-40 freeway. More than the other Route 66 towns in the eastern half of Arizona, it still feels like a real place, with lively cafés and some endearing roadside attractions around the center of town, where Route 66 alternates between Hopi Drive and Navajo Boulevard. Along with the many rock shops—be sure to check out the huge dinosaur collection outside the **Rainbow Rock Shop,** a block south on Navajo Boulevard near the railroad tracks—and trading post tourist traps, another worthwhile place to stop is the **Navajo County Historical Museum** (daily, free) in the old Navajo County Courthouse, about a quarter-mile south of I-40 at the corner of Navajo Boulevard (old Route 66) and Arizona Street. The collections are wide-ranging and include a walk downstairs to the old county jail, in use from 1899 until 1976 (the graffiti is great).

Best of all, stop for the night at the marvelous **Wigwam Village Motel** (811 W. Hopi Dr., 928/524-3048, around $55) at the western edge of town and sleep in a concrete tepee. Based on the original circa-1936 Wigwam Village motor court built in Cave City, Kentucky, Holbrook's was one of seven franchises across the country; this one opened in 1950 but closed down when the Interstate came through in 1974. The family of original owner Chester Lewis fully renovated the buildings and reopened the place after his death in 1988. Original bentwood hickory furniture, a small curio shop, and a handful of historic American cars parked outside help complete the ambience of classic roadside Americana. Especially if you want to introduce the younger generations to the joys of old-road travel, you really should stay here at least once in your life.

After you've checked in to the Wigwam, be sure to wander down the road for a friendly, filling Route 66 meal at **Joe and Aggie's Cafe** (120 W. Hopi Dr., 928/524-6540) or **The Wayside** (1150 W. Hopi Dr., 928/524-3167), serving delicious green-chile cheeseburgers and other Mexican and American favorites a mile west on old Route 66.

Winslow

Winslow, Arizona, didn't make it into Bobby Troup's original Route 66 hit list, but the town more than made it a generation later when Glenn Frey and the Eagles recorded the Jackson Browne tune "Take It Easy," whose second verse starts with "Standin' on a corner in Winslow, Arizona," a line that has caused more people to turn off in search of the place than anything else. Right downtown in between the two strips of Route 66, which runs one-way in each direction down 2nd and 3rd Streets, the funky **Old Trails Museum** (212 Kinsley Ave., 928/289-5861, Tues.-Sat., free) sells a range of "Standin' on the Corner" T-shirts, and displays a few reminders of Winslow in its heyday. Standing on the corner of 2nd and Kinsley, where a little sign stakes a claim to being *the* corner the Eagles sang about, there's a statue of a guy with a guitar and a mural of a girl (my lord!) in a flatbed Ford, slowing down to take a look.

I-40 and old Route 66 trace the southern edge of the massive Navajo Nation Indian Reservation, home to radio station **KTNN 660 AM,** which broadcasts a fascinating mélange of Navajo chants and Jimi Hendrix riffs on a "clear" signal that (especially at night) reaches all over the western USA. KTNN is also the only station in the United States that broadcasts pro football games—in Navajo.

The usual chain motels and fast-food franchises stand at either end of town around Winslow's I-40 exits, but in between is a great landmark of Southwest style: the elegant **La Posada Hotel** (303 E. 2nd St., 928/289-4366, $120 and up). Designed in the late 1920s for Fred Harvey by architect Mary Colter, who considered it her masterpiece, the hotel was closed for 40 years before being fully and lovingly restored and reopened in 1998. Near a busy rail line but surrounded by very pleasant gardens, the luxurious hotel is also home to a stylish cocktail bar and one of the finest restaurants for miles, the Turquoise Room. If you have the time and inclination to appreciate its old-fashioned, handcrafted charms, La Posada is an unforgettable stop.

Meteor Crater

Between Winslow and Winona, three miles east of Two Guns and six miles south of I-40 exit 233, sits **Meteor Crater** (928/289-5898, daily, $18), Arizona's second-most-distinctive hole in the ground. Formed by a meteorite some 50,000 years ago and mea-

suring 550 feet deep and nearly a mile across, the crater is a
privately owned tourist attraction. The Astronaut Wall of
Fame plays up the crater's re-
semblance to the surface of
the moon (Apollo moon-walk-
ers practiced here). You can't
climb down into it, but
(weather permitting) you can

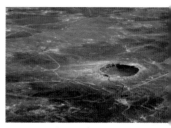

aerial view of Meteor Crater

join a guided rim tour, walking a half mile there and back across
the desert to gaze down into the crater.

Two Guns and Twin Arrows

Heading west from Meteor Crater toward Flagstaff, the route
climbs swiftly from the hot red desert up into the cool green pines.
Old-road fanatics will want to take the time to explore what remains of two old-time tourist traps lining the next 20 miles of
highway. Keep your eyes peeled approaching I-40 exit 230: The
freeway crosses deep Diablo Canyon, where an old Route 66 bridge
still spans the dry wash, and the walls of a half dozen bleached
buildings are all that's left of the **Two Guns Trading Post.** A roadside attraction par excellence, Two Guns had a zoo full of roadrun-
ners, Gila monsters, and coyotes, and one building still has a sign
saying Mountain Lions—all for the entertainment of passing travelers. For a while in the 1970s, Two Guns was a KOA Kampground
(with swimming pool!), and according to various reports down the
Route 66 grapevine, Two Guns has been on the verge of reopening
many times, most recently after reports circulated that the whole
shebang had been purchased by Australian actor Russell Crowe so
that he could film a remake of the classic Yul Brynner film
Westworld. But most of the time Two Guns is dead quiet, with the
old access road blocked by a sign reading "No Trespassing by Order
of Two Guns Sheriff Department." Probably a good thing, since the
old buildings are all dangerously close to collapse. It's an evocative
site, nonetheless, and photogenic in the right light.

A dozen miles west of Two Guns is another double attraction:
Twin Arrows, where a pair of giant and surprisingly well-preserved
red and yellow arrows point toward a long-closed café and trading
post, last seen alive in the 1990s movie *Forrest Gump.*

Twin Arrows is also home to the Navajo-owned **Twin Arrows
Casino Resort** (928/856-7200, $99 and up), the largest and most
expensive ($130+ million!) of the four casinos the tribe runs. Now

GET YOUR KICKS

If you ever plan to motor west
Travel my way, that's the highway that's the best
Get your kicks on Route 66.
It winds from Chicago to L.A.
More than 2,000 miles all the way
Get your kicks on Route 66
Now you go through St. Looey, Joplin, Missouri
And Oklahoma City is mighty pretty.
You'll see Amarillo, Gallup, New Mexico,
Flagstaff, Arizona, don't forget Winona,
Kingman, Barstow, San Bernardino.
Won't you get hip to this timely tip:
When you make that California trip
Get your kicks on Route 66.
Get your kicks on Route 66.
—Bobby Troup

One of the most popular road songs ever written, and a prime force behind the international popularity of Route 66, **"Get Your Kicks on Route 66"** was penned by jazz musician Bobby Troup in 1946 while he was driving west to seek fame and fortune in Los Angeles. Troup consistently credited his former wife Cynthia, with whom he was traveling, for the half dozen words of the title and refrain. The rest of the song simply rattled off the rhyming place-names along the way, but despite its apparent simplicity, it caught the ear of Nat King Cole, who made it into a hit record and also established the pronunciation as "root" rather than "rout," as repeated in later renditions by everyone from Bob Wills to the Rolling Stones.

If you haven't heard the song for a while, there's a jazzy version by Bobby Troup himself, along with some lively Route 66-related songs, on the compilation CD, *The Songs of Route 66—Music from the All-American Highway,* available at souvenir stores en route.

if only they'd spend some of that money fixing up Route 66 landmarks, starting with those Twin Arrows . . .

Don't Forget: Winona

East of Flagstaff, in fact across most of eastern Arizona, following
old Route 66 can be a frustrating task, since much of the roadway
is blocked, discontinuous, torn
up, or all three. Unlike the long
stretches found in the western
half of the state, here the old
road exists only as short seg-
ments running through towns,
and most of the way you're
forced to follow the freeway,
stopping at exit after exit to get

on and off the old road. Among the places worth considering is the
one town mentioned out of sequence in the Route 66 song:
"Flagstaff, Arizona, don't forget Winona," which, alas, is now little
more than a name on the exit sign along I-40.

Walnut Canyon National Monument

The most easily accessible of the hundreds of different prehistoric
settlements all over the southwestern United States, **Walnut
Canyon National Monument** (928/526-3367, daily 9am-5pm,
8am-5pm in summer, $5) is also one of the prettiest places imagin-
able, with piñon pines and junipers clinging to the canyon walls,
and walnut trees filling the canyon floor. On the edge of the canyon, a small visitors center gives the historical background, but the
real interest lies below, on the short but very steep Island Trail,
which winds through cliff dwellings tucked into overhangs and
ledges 400 feet above the canyon floor. Winter storms sometimes
dislodge boulders that wipe out parts of the trail. Check with the
rangers to make sure the trail is open, and ask about weather,
water supplies, and other safety issues. The rim of Walnut Canyon
is nearly 7,000 feet above sea level, and the altitude can make the
climbing especially strenuous.

The entrance to the Walnut Canyon monument, which contains
some 300 identified archaeological sites, lies seven miles east of
Flagstaff, accessible from I-40 exit 204.

Flagstaff

An old railroad and lumber-mill town given a new lease on life by an
influx of students at Northern Arizona University, and by the usual

array of ski bums and mountain bikers attracted by the surrounding high mountain wilderness, **Flagstaff** (pop. 68,870) is an enjoyable, energetic town high up on the Colorado Plateau. The natural beauty of its forested location has meant that, compared to other Route 66 towns, Flagstaff was less affected by the demise of the old road. That said, it still takes pride in the past, notably in the form of the **Museum Club** (3404 E. Route 66, 928/526-9434), an old roadhouse brought back to life as a country-western nightclub and ad hoc nostalgia museum.

Way back in 1946, in his classic *A Guide Book to Highway 66*, Jack Rittenhouse wrote that "Cowboys and Indians can be seen in their picturesque dress on Flagstaff streets year-round," but these days he'd probably notice the lycra-clad cyclists who crowd into the college town's many cafés.

Along with a great but slowly shrinking range of classic neon signs, Flagstaff also has a pair of non-Route 66 related attractions. First and foremost of these stands high on a hill on the west side of downtown Flagstaff, reachable from the west end of Santa Fe Avenue (old Route 66): the **Lowell Observatory,** established in 1894 by Percival Lowell and best known as the place where, in 1930, the onetime planet Pluto was discovered. A **visitors center** (928/774-3358, daily, $12) has descriptions of the science behind what goes on here—spectroscopy, red shifts, and expanding universes, for example—and the old telescope, a 24-inch refractor, is open for viewings 8pm-9:30pm most nights in summer. Not exactly consistent with its neon-lit Route 66 reputation, Flagstaff has since the 1950s been

a pioneer in combating light pollution. To help preserve the dark sky at night, here at the observatory and also at the surrounding natural sights, Flagstaff has proclaimed itself the world's first (and so far only) "International Dark Sky City."

Flagstaff's other main draw, the **Museum of Northern Arizona** (928/774-5213, daily, $10), perches at the edge of a pine-forested canyon three miles northwest of downtown via US-180, the main road to the Grand Canyon. Extensive exhibits de-tail the vibrant cultures of northern Arizona, from prehistoric Puebloans to contemporary Hopi, Navajo, and Zuni.

Downtown Flagstaff has more than enough espresso bars—probably a half dozen within a two-block radius of the train station—to satisfy its many multiply-pierced, twentysomething residents. There are also ethnic restaurants specializing in Greek, Thai, German, or Indian cuisine, so finding suitable places to eat and drink will not be a problem. Grab a cup of good coffee, a pastry, or a sandwich at

the telescope that discovered Pluto, Lowell Observatory

Macy's European Coffeehouse & Bakery (14 S. Beaver St., 928/774-2243), a cozy café two blocks north of the Northern Arizona University campus, or wander two blocks farther north and east, past the train station and across Route 66 to **MartAnne's Burrito Palace** (112 E. Route 66, 928/773-4701), a very popular little hole-in-the-wall serving authentic Mexican specialties (*posole, chilaquiles,* etc.) alongside more Americanized palate-pleasers like burritos. Hungry road-food fans may prefer to cruise west down Route 66 to the authentic-feeling **Galaxy Diner** (931 W. Route 66, 928/774-2466), open since 1959.

Step back into an even earlier time and stay at the classy (and possibly haunted) railroad-era **Hotel Monte Vista** (100 N. San Francisco St., 928/779-6971, $65-175), right off old Route 66. It was good enough for Gary Cooper, and it has been restored to its Roaring '20s splendor. For value and convenience, top marks go to the **Budget Inn** (913 S Milton Rd., 928/774-5038, $75 and up); it's a block south of Route 66, behind the Galaxy Diner. Accommodations are plentiful; if you can't decide, pick the motel with the most appealing sign.

Sunset Crater

While 90 percent of visitors approach the Grand Canyon from the south, a better and less crowded approach follows US-89 and Hwy-64, climbing up from the Navajo Nation deserts onto the Kaibab Plateau. The views are amazing in any direction—north across the desiccated Colorado Plateau, east across the colorful Painted

Desert, west to the forests of the Kaibab Plateau, or south to the angular San Francisco Peaks, including 12,663-foot Mount Humphreys, the highest point in Arizona.

This route is somewhat longer than the US-180 route to the Grand Canyon, but in most other ways it's far superior—not least because it gives access to a huge variety of scenery and historic sites. The first of these, 12 miles north of Flagstaff and 4 miles east of US-89, is **Sunset Crater,** a 1,000-foot-tall black basalt cone tinged with streaks of oranges and reds and capped by a sulfur-yellow rim—hence the name, which was bestowed by explorer John Wesley Powell in 1892. You can hike through the lava field that surrounds the cone, but the cone itself is off limits.

Sunset Crater marks the start of a scenic loop that winds around for some 30 miles through neighboring **Wupatki National Monument** (928/679-2365, daily, $5). The monument protects the remains of a prehistoric Native American community, thought to have been ancestors of the Hopi, who lived here between AD 1100 and 1225 and now inhabit the broad mesas rising to the northeast. Hundreds of ruins—most in very fine condition—are spread over the 35,000-acre monument. The largest ruin, 100-room **Tall House,** stands near a ceremonial amphitheater and a very rare ball court, which may indicate a link with the Mayan cultures of Central America.

Back on US-89, 20 miles north of the north entrance to Wupatki, the crossroads settlement of **Cameron** stands at the junction with Hwy-64, which heads up (and up) to the east entrance of **Grand Canyon National Park.** A mile north of the Hwy-64 junction, along the

Flagstaff's San Francisco Street was named not for the California city but for the nearby volcanic peaks, so called by early Spanish missionaries and still held sacred by the native Hopi Indians.

Flagstaff very nearly became an early movie center, when young Cecil B. DeMille stopped here briefly while scouting locations to shoot the world's first feature-length film, a Western called *The Squaw Man.* It was snowing in Flagstaff that day, so he moved on to Los Angeles.

Cameron is named in memory of a cantankerous prospector-turned-early-promoter of the Grand Canyon. Ralph Cameron blazed the Bright Angel Trail (then charged tourists $1 to use it) and did everything he could to obstruct the government from taking over "his" canyon—even going so far as to get elected U.S. senator (in 1920) so he could try to eliminate the newly established national park.

south bank of the Little Colorado River is historic **Cameron Trading Post** (800/338-7385, $70-110), which includes a motel and an RV park. It stands next to an equally historic one-lane suspension bridge, built in 1911 (and now carrying an oil pipeline). Cameron makes a good alternative to Tusayan, in case all the Grand Canyon's in-park accommodations are full.

From Cameron, Hwy-64 runs west along the Little Colorado River Gorge, which Hopi cosmology considers to be the place where man emerged into the present world. This deep canyon leads into the much larger Grand Canyon, while Hwy-64 climbs up the plateau for 30 miles to the east entrance of Grand Canyon National Park. Your first overlook is a desert view, where the photogenic 1930s Watchtower gives a great taste of the canyon from the highest point on the South Rim.

Detour: Grand Canyon National Park

One of the wonders of the natural world, the **Grand Canyon** of the Colorado River—277 miles long, a mile deep, and anywhere from 5 to 18 miles across—defies description, and if you're anywhere nearby you really owe it to yourself to stop for a look. The most amazing thing about the Grand Canyon, apart from its sheer size and incredible variety of shapes and colors, is how different it looks when viewed from different places (artist David Hockney has said that the Grand Canyon is the only place on Earth that makes you want to look in all directions—up, down, and side to side—at the same time). Be sure to check it out from as many angles, and at as many different times of day, as you can. A book like this one can do little more than hint at all there is to see and do, but if you have

view of the Grand Canyon looking to the North Rim
including Bright Angel Trail

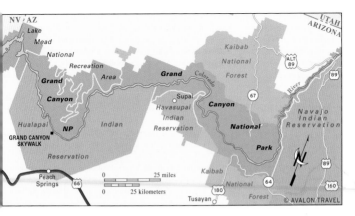

time for nothing else, take a quick hike down into the canyon to get a real sense of its truly awesome scale.

The great majority of the nearly five million people who visit the Grand Canyon each year arrive at the **South Rim** and gaze down into the Grand Canyon from **Mather Point,** where the entrance road hits the edge of the gorge. The park visitors center and most of the food and lodging are located a mile west at **Grand Canyon Village.** Beyond Grand Canyon Village, **West Rim Drive** winds west, leading past the **J. W. Powell Memorial** at Hopi Point (from where you get great views of the Colorado River, which otherwise can be surprisingly hard to see) and a series of other viewpoints before ending up at **Hermit's Rest,** eight miles from Grand Canyon Village—where there are yet more stupendous views as well as restrooms, drinking fountains, and a gift shop.

The West Rim Drive, which was built for tourists by the Santa Fe Railroad in 1912, is closed to cars throughout summer, but frequent shuttle buses stop at all the viewpoints. A six-mile hiking trail runs west from the Powell Memorial to Hermit's Rest, and a three-mile paved nature trail links the Powell Memorial with Grand Canyon Village.

East from Mather Point, **East Rim Drive** runs for 25 miles, stopping first at aptly named **Grandview Point,** 12 miles from Grand Canyon Village and a half mile north of the East Rim Drive. This is, literally and figuratively, a high point of any Grand Canyon tour, giving a 270-degree panorama over the entire gorge. Continuing east, the road passes a small prehistoric pueblo at **Tusayan Ruins** before ending with a bang at **Desert View Watchtower,** an Anasazi-style tower set right at the edge of the canyon. Though it looks ancient, the tower was created for tourists in 1932, designed by Mary

Colter, also the architect of the Bright Angel Lodge and most of the wonderful old Harvey House hotels that lined Route 66 across the Southwest.

From the watchtower, the road continues along the rim through the east entrance, then drops down to the cross-roads town of Cameron and the Little Colorado River.

Grand Canyon Hikes

To get a real feel for the Grand Canyon, you have to get out of the car, get beyond the often overcrowded viewpoints that line the South Rim, and take a walk down into the depths of the canyon itself. The most popular and best-maintained path, the **Bright Angel Trail,** descends from the west end of Grand Canyon Village, following a route blazed by prospectors in the 1890s. It's an 18-mile hike down to the Colorado River and back. There are rest stops (with water) along the way; however, the park does not recommend anyone walking from rim to river in one day. A shorter day hike cuts off to **Plateau Point,** 1,300 feet above the river and a 13-mile round-trip from the South Rim. If you can finagle a reservation, you can stay overnight at **Phantom Ranch,** on the north side of the Colorado River, which is accessed from the South Rim by a pair of suspension bridges. Camping at nearby **Bright Angel Campground,** which has space for more than 100 people, requires an advance permit from the park. Permit information is available at www.nps.gov/grca or by calling the main visitors center for details.

Another interesting old trail drops down from Grandview Point to **Horseshoe Mesa,** where you can still see the remnants of an old copper mine that closed in 1907. This is a six-mile round-trip and gives an unforgettable introduction to the Grand Canyon.

No matter where you go, when hiking down into the canyon remember that it will take you twice as long to hike back up again, that the rim can be covered in snow and ice as late as June, and *always carry water*—especially in summer—at least a quart for every hour you're on the trail. The very good **visitors center** (928/638-7888)) in Grand Canyon Village has information about the park's

Lower Ribbon Falls

many hiking trails, the canyon's geology, the burro rides that take you down and back up again, and anything else to do with the Grand Canyon.

Practicalities

It may give a sense of the immensity of the Grand Canyon to know that, while the North Rim is a mere 6-10 miles from the South Rim as the crow flies, to get there by road requires a drive of at least 215 miles.

Most of what you'll need to know to enjoy your Grand Canyon visit is contained in the brochure you're given at the entrance, where you pay the $25-per-car fee (national parks passes are accepted).

To make advance reservations for accommodations—a good idea at any time of year but essential in the peak summer months—phone the park concessionaire, **Xanterra** (303/297-2757 or 888/297-2757 in advance, 928/638-2631 for same-day cancellations), which handles reservations for the six very different lodges in Grand Canyon Village. The most characterful and best-value place to stay is the **Bright Angel Lodge,** which overlooks the canyon; the cheapest rooms share bathrooms, while others have canyon views and fireplaces. The coffee shop here is open all day, there's a pretty nifty soda fountain right on the edge of the canyon, and the lobby fireplace shows off the rock strata, in proper chronological order, that form the walls of the Grand Canyon. The other historic lodge is the **El Tovar Hotel,** built in 1905 but recently renovated; rooms here start around $200 and top out at more than $400 a night. The El Tovar also has the park's best restaurant—and a comfy piano bar to help while away the night.

For a basic motel bed, there are four other lodges in Grand Canyon Village, offering more than 750 rooms altogether, costing $90-210 a night. There's also a very nice lodge at the North Rim, open usually mid-May to mid-October.

It's more of an effort to reach, but the best place to get a feel for the Grand Canyon is splendid **Phantom Ranch,** a rustic complex of cabins and dormitories way down in the canyon, on the north side of the Colorado River. Space here is usually taken up by people on overnight burro-ride packages (which cost around $400). But, particularly in the off-season, you may be able to get a bed without the standard six months (or more) advance reservation. Ask at the desk in the Bright Angel Lodge, or call 303/297-2757.

Reservations for **camping** (877/444-6777 or online at www.recreation.gov) at the South Rim are also essential in summer. The largest facility, **Mather Campground** (no hookups, $18 a night), is near Market Plaza, the park's general store and commerce area, and is open year-round, with more than 300 sites and coin-operated showers. Sites with RV hookups are available nearby at the Xanterra-run **Trailer Village.** There's another National Park Service campground at **Desert View,** near the east entrance. Backcountry camping (overnight permits required) is available at established sites down in the canyon.

If all the in-park accommodations are full, thousands of rooms are available in Williams, Flagstaff, and right outside the park's southern boundary at **Tusayan,** where you can choose from a Best Western, a Holiday Inn Express, and a Quality Inn.

Williams

The last Route 66 town to be bypassed by I-40, **Williams** (pop. 2,842; elev. 6,780 feet) held out until the bitter end, waging court battle after court battle before finally surrendering on October 13, 1984. Despite the town's long opposition, in the end Williams gave in gracefully, going so far as to hold a celebration-cum-wake for the old road, high-

lighted by a performance atop a new freeway overpass by none other than Mr. Route 66 himself, Bobby "Get Your Kicks" Troup.

Williams today is primarily a gateway to the Grand Canyon, but it also takes full tourist advantage of its Route 66 heritage: The downtown streets sport old-fashioned street lamps, and every other store sells a variety of Route 66 souvenirs, making the town much more than a pit stop for Grand Canyon-bound travelers. Apart from the Route 66 connections, Williams's pride and joy is the vintage **Grand Canyon Railway** (800/843-8724, round-trip costs around $70), which whistles and steams its way north to the canyon every morning, taking roughly two hours each way. Call for current schedules and fares, or stop by the historic depot, a former Harvey House hotel restored in 1990.

If you hanker after a slice of pie and a cup of coffee, or simply appreciate good food and a warm welcome, you'll want to save time and space for the **Pine Country Restaurant** (107 N. Grand Canyon

Grand Canyon Railway

Blvd., 928/635-9718), serving breakfast, lunch, dinner, and famous fresh pies near the train station. Williams is also home to a landmark old Route 66 restaurant, **Rod's Steak House** (301 E. Route 66, 928/635-2671), in business since 1946. Just south of Route 66 there's a very popular **Singing Pig BBQ Restaurant** (106 S. 3rd St., 928/635-2904).

For a place to stay—and there are many, thanks to the nearby Grand Canyon—there are a couple of old motor court motels, one disguised as an **EconoLodge** (302 E. Route 66, 928/635-4085, $90 and up), another branded as a **Rodeway Inn** (928/635-4041, $110 and up). At the upper end of the scale, try the plushly renovated **Lodge on Route 66** (200 E. Route 66, 877/563-4366, $100 and up), or look into that historic Harvey House hotel, now known as the **Grand Canyon Railway Hotel** (800/843-8724, $170 and up), a very plush overnight that's ideal for passengers taking the vintage train to the Grand Canyon.

Sedona

Most Arizona visitors head for the Grand Canyon, but smaller and still scenic **Oak Creek Canyon,** just south of Flagstaff, has one great advantage over its world-famous neighbor: You can drive through it, on scenic Hwy-89A. Starting right at the edge of Flagstaff, this red sandstone gorge has been cut into the surrounding pine and juniper forests by eons of erosion. The most popular place to enjoy Oak Creek Canyon, **Slide Rock State Park** (928/282-3034, daily, $20), 18 miles south of Flagstaff and 7 miles north of Sedona, is a 55-acre, day-use-only area focused on the long, natural rock chute for which the park is named. Nearby **Slide Rock Lodge** (928/282-3531, around $130) has peaceful motel rooms. No Wi-Fi is provided, but there are barbecue grills for the do-it-yourself cook.

At the south end of Oak Creek Canyon, 25 miles from Flagstaff, the otherworldly landscape surrounding **Sedona** (pop. 10,031) has made it one of the nation's most popular vacation destinations, particularly for New Agey visitors, who in the past 20 years have made Sedona into an upmarket center for psychic channeling, soul travel, and

Cathedral Rock

the like. Sedona first came to attention in the 1950s, when the red-rock spires that dominate the local landscape were seen in a wide variety of Hollywood westerns (including *Johnny Guitar*). Despite the rampant sprawl—and the high hotel rates, which can reach $200 a night—Sedona is still well worth a look, especially if you can get away from the town and explore some of the surrounding wilderness.

Jerome

South of Route 66 and I-40 from Ash Fork, or west from Sedona, Hwy-89A makes a wonderfully scenic loop, winding past 7,815-foot Mingus Mountain into photogenic **Jerome** (pop. 378; elev. 5,400 feet), the liveliest and most interesting "ghost town" in Arizona. Set on steep streets that switchback up the mountainside, Jerome is an old copper mining camp that has turned itself into a thriving artists' community, with many nice shops, galleries, and cafés, and almost no touristy schlock. Park wherever you can and walk around, enjoying the incredible views out over the Verde Valley to the San Francisco Peaks and beyond.

At the north (uphill) edge of town, a mile off Hwy-89 at the end of fairly rough Perkinsville Road, the **Gold King Mine** (928/634-0053, daily 10am-5pm, $5) has a misleading name but is still a great place to go. It's not so much a mine as an anarchic collection of ancient-looking machinery (sawmills, pumps, hoists, trucks, cars, and ore cars), most of which is kept in working order, plus an intact old gas station dating from Jerome's 1920s heyday.

At the heart of Jerome, enjoy food or a fine shot of espresso at the **Flatiron Cafe** (416 Main St., 928/634-2733), or for a full meal with a great view, try the delicious Asylum dining room inside the huge old **Jerome Grand Hotel** (200 Hill St., 928/634-8200, $125 and up), a former hospital.

Seligman

From I-40 exit 139, just west of Ash Fork, a very nice section of the old Route 66 two-lane runs along the railroad tracks just north of, and parallel to, the I-40 freeway all the way to the sleep little town of Seligman. One of best places to stop and get a feel for the spirit of old Route 66, **Seligman** (pop. 510; pronounced "SLIG-man") is a perfect place to take a break before or after rejoining the Interstate hordes. The town retains a lot of its historic character—old sidewalk awnings and even a few hitching rails—and offers lots of reasons to stop. Coming into Seligman on this stretch of Route 66, you'll be greeted by **The Rusty Bolt** (115 Route 66, 928/422-0106), a fantastic junk shop and oddball emporium that's impossible to miss along the north side of the old highway. A pilgrimage point for old-roads fans for decades, Angel Delgadillo's barber shop now hosts the **Route 66 Gift Shop and Museum** (217 E. Route 66). Angel's brother, Juan Delgadillo, created and ran the wacky **Snow Cap Drive-In** (301 E. Route 66, 928/422-3291) a half block to the east, where the sign says "Sorry, We're Open," and the menu advertises "Hamburgers without Ham." Behind the restaurant, in snow, rain, or shine, sits a roofless old Chevy decorated with fake flowers and an artificial Christmas tree. Juan's family carries on the Snow Cap traditions. The burgers, fries, and milk shakes (not to mention the jokes!) are worth driving miles for.

Another very good place to eat is the kitschy **Road Kill Café** (502 W. Route 66, 928/422-3554) near the OK Saloon and Rusty Bolt junk shop. Find German-American barbecue at **Westside Lilo's** (415 W. Route 66, 928/422-5456); good coffee served behind the bright-green facade of **Seligman Sundries,** a half mile farther west; and the cold beer typically downed by cowboys and truckers across the road at the **Black Cat Bar.**

For an overnight, choose from a half dozen motels like the nice, clean, and friendly **Historic Route 66 Motel** (22750 W. Route 66, 928/422-3204, $75 and up).

Delgadillo's Snow Cap

Just west of the Grand Canyon Caverns, Hwy-18 cuts off 65 miles to the northeast toward the **Havasupai Indian Reservation,** which includes one of the most beautiful and untrammeled corners of the Grand Canyon. No roads, just red rocks, green canyons, cobalt-blue waterfalls, and the **Havasupai Lodge** (928/448-2111, $145 and up).

The longest and probably the most evocative stretch of old Route 66 runs between Seligman and Kingman through the high-desert **Hualapai Reservation** (pronounced "WALL-ah-pie"), along the Santa Fe Railroad tracks through all-but-abandoned towns bypassed by the "modern" Interstate world. Save the stretch between here and Needles for daytime, as it's one of the most memorable of the Mother Road's whole cross-country haul.

Grand Canyon Caverns

Far, far away from the high-speed freeway frontage, midway between Williams and Kingman, 22 miles northwest of Seligman and a dozen miles east of Peach Springs, a large green sign marks the entrance to **Grand Canyon Caverns** (928/422-3223, daily, $20-70), which has somehow managed to survive despite being bypassed by the I-40 superslab. Once one of the prime tourist draws on the Arizona stretch of Route 66, the Grand Canyon Caverns were discovered and developed in the late 1920s and still have the feel of an old-time roadside attraction. Tours start every half hour at the gift shop, where you hop on the elevator that drops you 200 feet to underground chambers, including the 18,000-square-foot Chapel of the Ages. Tours last around 45 minutes. Back above ground, there's also a gas station and a motel. If you want a truly unique experience, ask about staying overnight in the **Cave Suite,** a fully furnished two-bed suite dating back to the 1962 Cuban Missile Crisis, when a corner of the caverns was set up as a fallout shelter.

Old Route 66 Loop: Grand Canyon Skywalk

Midway along the Historic Route 66 loop between Seligman and Kingman, the road comes close to the Grand Canyon as it passes through the large and lonely Hualapai Indian Reservation. The 2,100-strong Hualapai tribe has its community center at the town of **Peach Springs,** which marks the halfway point of this 90-mile, old-roads loop and offers at least one reason to stop: the comfortable **Hualapai Lodge** (928/769-2636, $70 and up) and Diamond Creek restaurant, right on Route 66. Apart from this, Peach

Grand Canyon Skywalk

Springs is mostly a prefab Bureau of Indian Affairs housing project with few services, though there is a photogenic old Route 66 filling station at the center of town.

The lodge was the first sign of tourism in Peach Springs, but the Hualapai tribe seems to have embraced commerce in a big way: 2007 saw the opening of the much-hyped (and much-troubled) **Grand Canyon Skywalk,** a glass-floored steel horseshoe that juts out from the edge of the Grand Canyon, 4,000 feet higher than the Colorado River. Installed at a cost of $30 million, the very daring and impressive Skywalk is certainly unique, but it's also very expensive (count on it costing close to $80 per person, including lots of annoying fees and charges to park and ride the bus out to the Skywalk itself). The Skywalk is most popular as a day-trip destination from Las Vegas, but you can get here from Peach Springs via 78 miles of rough roads. The recommended route is to take I-40 or Route 66 to Kingman (50 miles southwest of Peach Springs), then head north via US-93, Pierce Ferry Road, and Diamond Bar Road, sections of which are still unpaved.

A museum is planned and facilities are supposed to start being improved once the money rolls in, but for now there isn't much apart from the Skywalk itself. There's an ambitious long-term plan to develop the entire western end of the Hualapai Reservation into "Grand Canyon West," with all sorts of water-

Peach Springs is the starting point for the 19-mile drive along Diamond Creek Road—all the way to the "bottom" of the Grand Canyon. Get a permit and detailed info at the Hualapai Lodge.

rafting tours and outdoor activities on offer; time will tell if the Skywalk endures once the novelty wears off.

West of Peach Springs, Route 66 winds along the railroad tracks, passing through a few ghost towns (like Hackberry, where the old gas station still stands in rusting splendor) before zooming into Kingman.

Kingman

The only town for miles in any direction since its founding as a railroad center in 1880, **Kingman** (pop. 27,521) has always depended upon passing travelers for its livelihood. Long a main stopping place on Route 66, and still providing the only all-night services on US-93 between Las Vegas and Phoenix, and along I-40 between Flagstaff and Needles, the town remains more a way station than a destination despite the increasing number of people who have relocated here in recent years, attracted by the open space, high desert air, and low cost of living.

The best first stop in Kingman is **The Powerhouse** (120 W. Andy Devine Ave., 928/753-9889, $4), a hulking old power plant that's been inventively reused to house a very good Route 66 museum, with galleries full of enough old cars, postcards, and mementos to occupy you for an hour or more. Best of the bunch is a nifty relief map of the entire path of Route 66 (the many mountain ranges make you realize why old cars needed so many service stations!).

The stretch of Route 66 through Kingman has been renamed in memory of favorite son Andy Devine, who was born in Flagstaff in 1905 but grew up here, where his parents ran the Beale Hotel. One of the best-known character actors of Hollywood's classic era, the raspy-voiced Devine usually played a devoted sidekick. His most famous role was as the wagon driver in the classic 1939 John Ford western *Stagecoach*.

The displays do a good job of evoking and exploring the deep romance many Americans seem to feel for the old Mother Road.

Be sure to contact the **visitors center** (928/753-6106) here to pick up a copy of the town's very good Route 66 brochure. Then pop across Route 66 for a burger, some fries, and a milk shake at the very good **Mr. D'z Route 66 Diner** (105 E. Andy Devine Ave., 928/718-0066), impossible to miss thanks to its bank of neon.

The blocks off Route 66 hold Kingman's most interesting older buildings—Beale Street, north of Route 66, has dozens of 100-year-old railroad era storefronts now housing an array of junk and antiques shops.

Besides the usual chain motels along I-40, accommodation options in Kingman include the pleasant **Hill Top Motel** (1901 E. Andy Devine Ave., 928/753-2198, $45 and up), forever infamous as the place where evil Timothy McVeigh stayed for a week before blowing up the Federal Building in Oklahoma City.

To escape the summer heat, Kingmanites head east and south along a well-marked 14-mile road to **Hualapai Mountain Park,** where pines and firs cover the slopes of the 8,417-foot peak. Hiking trails wind through the wilderness, where there's a campground and a few rustic **cabins** ($65-130) built by the Civilian Conservation Corps during the New Deal 1930s. Contact the **ranger station** (928/757-0915) near the park entrance for detailed information or to make reservations.

Cool Springs and Black Mountains

Midway between Kingman and Oatman, set against the angular **Black Mountains** high above the desert plain, **Cool Springs** is a nifty old rough stone service station resurrected as a Route 66 gift shop and mini museum. Built in the 1920s, abandoned in the 1960s, and brought back to life in 2005, Cool Springs is a nice place to stop, buy a soda, and soak up the Route 66 spirit.

Between Cool Springs and Oatman, old Route 66 twists and turns past recently reactivated gold mine workings while climbing up and over the angular Black Mountains. Steep switchbacks and 15-mph hairpin turns carry the old road on a breathtaking 2,100-foot change in elevation over a very short eight miles of blacktop.

Old Route 66: Oatman

One of the most demanding, desolate, and awesomely satisfying stretches of the old road loops north from the I-40 freeway, between Kingman and the California border. Climbing over steep mountains while cutting across a stretch of desert that brings new meaning to the word "harsh," the narrow roadway passes few signs of life on this 50-mile loop, so be sure you and your car are prepared for the rigors of desert driving.

Crossing the Colorado River between Arizona and California, look downstream (south) from the I-40 freeway to see the arching silver steel bridge that carried Route 66 up until 1966. It's still in use, supporting a natural gas pipeline; beyond it, the red-rock spires for which Needles is named rise sharply out of the desert plains.

Westbound drivers have it the easiest—simply follow the well-signed Historic Route 66 west from Kingman, exit 44 off I-40. From the west heading east, take exit 1 on the Arizona side of the

LONDON BRIDGE

It may not have stood out as the finest piece of engineering art when it spanned the Thames, but London Bridge is a marvelous sight in the middle of the Arizona desert. A replacement for a series of bridges that date back to medieval times, inspiring the children's rhyme, "London Bridge Is Falling Down," this version of London Bridge was constructed in the 1830s. When it was no longer able to handle the demands of London traffic, the old bridge was replaced by a modern concrete span and its stones were put up for sale in 1967.

Bought by property developer Robert McCulloch for $2.4 million, the 10,246 blocks of stone were shipped here and reassembled at a cost of another $7 million. After a channel was cut under the bridge to bring water from the Colorado River, the Lord Mayor of London flew in to attend the rededication ceremonies in October 1971. The bridge now stands as the centerpiece of a fast-growing retirement and resort community that's home to more than 50,000 residents.

There's no admission charge to see this oddly compelling sight. If you have a taste for surreal experiences, walk across the bridge and sample the Ye Olde England ambience of Barley Brothers brewpub. Even more schizoid is the adjacent, all-suite **London Bridge Resort** (866/331-9231, $125 and up), where the "original" medieval turrets and Arthurian design flourishes have been redecorated with palm trees for that unforgettable tropical island experience.

river, then head north. Whichever way you go, you can't avoid the steep hills that lead to **Oatman** (elev. 2,700 feet), an odd mix of ghost town and tourist draw that's one of the top stops along Route 66. A gold mining town whose glory days had long faded by the time I-40 passed it by way back in 1952, Oatman looks like a Wild West stage set, but it's the real thing—awnings over the plank sidewalks, bearded roughnecks (and a few burros) wandering the streets, lots of rust, and slumping old buildings. The gold mines here produced some two million ounces from their start in

1904 until they panned out in the mid-1930s; at its peak, Oatman had a population of over 10,000, with 20 saloons lining the three-block Main Street. One of these, the old **Oatman Hotel** (181 N. Main St.), was where Clark Gable and Carole Lombard were said to have spent their first night after getting married in Kingman in 1939. You can sample some highly recommended Navajo tacos and have a beer in the downstairs bar (which is thickly wallpapered in years and years worth of dollar bills!), or peer through a Plexiglas door at the room where Clark and Carole slept, hardly changed for half a century.

The crossing over the Colorado River at the California/Arizona border was the site of illegal but effective roadblocks during the Dust Bowl era, when vigilante mobs turned back migrant Okies if they didn't have much money.

Saloons and T-shirt shops line the rest of Main Street, where Wild West enthusiasts act out the shootouts that took place here only in the movies. Oatman does get a considerable tourist trade, but after dark and outside of the peak summer tourist season, the town reverts to its rough-and-tumble ways. The conservative, libertarian bent of most of the local population ensures that nothing is likely to change Oatman's crusty charms.

Lake Havasu City

The first stop east of the Colorado River, just across the state border and 23 miles south of I-40, **Lake Havasu City** is a thoroughly modern vacation town built around a thoroughly odd centerpiece: **London Bridge,** brought here stone by stone between 1967 and 1971. Terribly tacky souvenir shops and faux London pubs congregate around the foot of the bridge, which spans a manmade channel to a large island, but the bridge itself is an impressive sight.

Unless you plan to retire here—or simply rent a houseboat and relax on the water—there's not a lot to do at Lake Havasu. That said, the area has become a popular spring break destination for western college kids, thousands of whom flock to **Lake Havasu State Park** (928/855-2784) for fun-in-the-sun and who-knows-what after dark. For the rest of us—have an English muffin and a cup of tea, pay your respects and take a photograph or two, then hit the road again.

CALIFORNIA

From the demanding **Mojave Desert,** over mountains and through lush inland valleys, to the beautiful beaches of **Santa Monica,** Route 66 passes through every type of Southern California landscape. The old road, which survives intact almost all the way across the state, is marked for most of its 315 miles by signs declaring it Historic Route 66. Across the Mojave Desert the route is also marked as the National Old Trails Highway, its title before the national numbering system was put into effect in the late 1920s.

Needles

Founded soon after the Santa Fe Railroad came through in 1883 and named for the group of sharp stone spires that stand near where I-40 crosses the Colorado River from Arizona, **Needles** (pop. 4,844) is one of the hottest places in the country, with summertime highs hovering between 100°F and 120°F for months on end. Though often unbearable in summer, Needles is a popular place with winter snowbirds escaping colder climes; it also has a very rich Route 66 heritage. The stretch of old Route 66 through Needles runs along Broadway, alternating along both sides of the freeway. The magnificent El Garces Hotel is undergoing long-term renovation into a restaurant, hotel, historical museum, and visitors center. Until it is back open for business, the best place to stop and soak some Route 66 personality is the **Wagon Wheel Restaurant** (2420 Needles Hwy., 760/326-4305), west of downtown, open all day for good, fresh food, and on Friday nights for all-you-can-eat fish 'n' chips.

Needles was the boyhood home of *Peanuts* cartoonist Charles Schulz and is featured in the comic strips as the desert home of Snoopy's raffish sibling, Spike. Needles now features Spike and Snoopy in a series of Route 66-themed murals around town, as at the gas station on Needles Highway.

If you're set on traveling as much of the old road as possible, another stretch of Route 66 runs west of Needles and north of I-40 through the near-ghost towns of **Goffs** and **Fenner,** on a roller coaster of undulating two-lane blacktop, parallel to the railroad tracks.

Old Route 66 Loop: Ludlow and Amboy

Thanks to the orderly planners of the Santa Fe Railroad, which first blazed this route across the desert in 1883, many of the place-names on this old Route 66 loop come in alphabetical order: from west to east, you have Amboy, Bristol, Cadiz, Danby, Essex, Fenner, Goffs, Home, Ibis, Java, and Klinefelter. Yes, Klinefelter.

From Needles, it's a quick 25-mile drive north along the Colorado River into Nevada to visit the gambling center of **Laughlin,** a sparkling city with huge casinos and over 10,000 cheap rooms.

If you want a quick and convincing taste of what traveling across the Mojave Desert was like in the days before air-conditioning and cellular phones, keep your eyes peeled for Historic Route 66 signs, and turn south off I-40 and follow the National Old Trails Highway, one of the many monikers Route 66 has carried over the years, on a 75-mile loop along the old road. Heading west, the loop leaves I-40 about 25 miles beyond Needles; heading east, the old road turns off I-40 at **Ludlow,** 50 miles east of Barstow, where two gas stations, a coffee shop, and a motel represent a major outpost of civilization.

While the drive alone is worth the extra time it takes, the real attraction comes midway along this old road loop: **Amboy** is synonymous with **Roy's Motel and Café,** a museum-worthy assembly of roadside architecture that has survived solely due to the willpower of its longtime lord and master, Buster Burris, who ran the place from 1938 (when he married the daughter of owner Roy Crowl) until 2000, when Buster died at the age of 92. In the late 1940s, Roy's was the prime stop between Needles and Barstow, and as many as 90 people staffed the café, the motel, and the car repair shop, working around the clock to cater to the thousands of passing cars. Roy's fell on hard times after the opening of I-40 in 1974, but the whole

town—complete with a huge "Roy's" sign, a set of simple motor court cabins, and a pair of gas pumps—has hung on. Now, thanks to owner Albert Okura (who also owns the San Bernardino-based restaurant chain Juan Pollo and the "First McDonald's" museum), Amboy is used as a film and photo-shoot location as well as being a photogenic reminder of the heyday of Route 66.

From Amboy, you can leave Route 66 and head south to the lovely high desert of **Joshua Tree National Park** and the newly re-energized, 1950s Rat Pack-era resorts of **Palm**

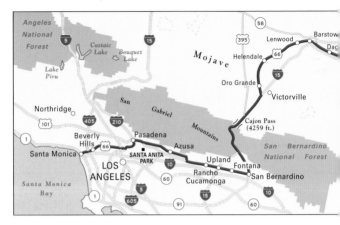

Springs. Staying on Route 66, you'll pass the lava flows around **Amboy Crater,** and you may see and hear helicopters and Warthog fighters playing war games on the huge **Twentynine Palms Marine Corps base,** which stretches off to the south. At nearly 1,000 square miles, it's the largest base in the country and often the last U.S. stop for personnel bound for battle in the Middle East.

Mojave National Preserve

Spreading north of old Route 66, more than 1.5 million acres between I-40 and I-15 have been set aside as the **Mojave National Preserve,** a harsh desert landscape of volcanic cinder cones and sand dunes, desert tortoises, and Joshua trees. One evocative landmark here in the middle of the desert is the **Kelso Depot** (760/252-6165), a restored train station that sits on the main L.A. to Las Vegas Union Pacific railroad line. Trains still rumble past, and the depot, featuring a variety of interpretive exhibits, re-creates the sense of life here in the 1920s, before air-conditioning and cell phones made life in the desert so much more agreeable. Kelso is on Kelbaker Road, about 22 miles north of I-40, midway between Fenner and Ludlow.

Huge chunks of the Mojave Desert have been used as military training grounds since World War II, when General George Patton commandeered this area to prepare his tank battalions for battle in the North African desert. The remains of the camp can still be seen in the desert along Crucero Road, just north of the I-40 Ludlow exit.

Another of the many places in the Mojave Preserve that's worth the trip is **Mitchell Caverns** (760/928-2586, $6) at the center of **Providence Mountains**

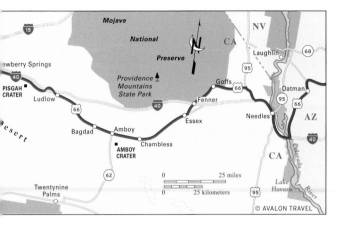

State Recreation Area, 25 miles north of I-40 at the end of Essex Road. At the time of this writing, the park was closed due to state budget cuts. Call before you make the drive.

> The Mojave Desert is one of the driest places on the planet. Parts of it receive less than three inches of rainfall in an average year, sometimes going for more than two years without getting a drop.

Newberry Springs: Bagdad Cafe

Running alongside the I-40 freeway for about 50 miles east of Barstow, old Route 66 survives as a sort of frontage road, passing little more than an occasional lava flow (like Pisgah Crater, where there's a pair of I-40 rest areas).

About 20 miles east of Barstow is the place that for many people symbolizes the quirky personality of Route 66: **Newberry Springs.** The cult classic Percy Adlon movie *Bagdad Cafe* was shot at the town's one and only café, now also known as the **Bagdad Cafe** (760/257-3101). Ccionsidering its connections with the oddly endearing movie (which features a cast of drifters, a fat German magician, and Jack Palance!), the real-life Bagdad Cafe is welcoming and appropriately weird, not so much a restaurant as it is a semi-catered film set. It stays in business as a pit stop for fans of offbeat European cinema who happen to find themselves in the middle of the Mojave Desert. Be sure to read and sign the guest book, which features heartfelt comments from hundreds of people who've made the trek here from all over the world. (Scandinavians and other Teutonic types seem especially well represented.)

Between the Bagdad Cafe and Barstow, old Route 66 runs past the region's other unique claim to fame: The semi-successful **Solar**

Detour: Las Vegas

Viva Las Vegas! Since its founding more than 100 years ago, Las Vegas has been the biggest, brightest, and brazenest boomtown in the history of the world. Even the ongoing recession and sub-prime real estate crash, which saw property values cut in half amidst the worldwide economic downturn, hasn't really dampened its spirits: In the past 40 years, the population has more than tripled, and over a dozen major hotels and mega-resorts have re-created everything from ancient Egypt to Venice (complete with canals and gondoliers), Paris (a mock Eiffel Tower), and New York City (with a Coney Island roller coaster and fake steam puffing up from fake sidewalks). More numbers: With more than 150,000 rooms, the city has as many as New York and Chicago combined, and 40 million annual visitors lose more than $8 billion in the casinos here every year.

In addition to gambling, Las Vegas casinos have all the rooms, restaurants, and "recreational opportunities" you can imagine (and then some). If you're staying overnight, you'll enter the wacky and somewhat wicked world of Las Vegas lodging. Rooms are no longer the dirt-cheap bargains they were a generation ago; rates vary depending on the time of year, time of the week, and sometimes even the time of day. Count on spending at least $100 for a decent hotel room, and close to five times that for something special. You should defi-

nitely make reservations as early as you can; on Friday nights, or during a big convention or boxing match, the whole town is often sold out. A final note: If you'll be schlepping a lot of luggage, be aware that Las Vegas hotel rooms are a very long way from their parking spaces, which are in huge high-rise or underground garages. On the upside, parking is free at most hotels.

Here are a few of the many places you can play:

Caesars Palace (3570 Las Vegas Blvd. S., 702/731-7110 or 866/227-5938): Long before there was a Mirage; a New York, New York; a Bellagio; or a Venetian, there was Caesars Palace. Though ancient by Las Vegas standards (Caesars opened in 1966 as the first "themed" hotel in Las Vegas), this is still one of the classiest and most famous places in town.

Hard Rock Hotel and Casino (4455 Paradise Rd., 702/693-5000 or 800/473-7625): For anyone under 60, this is the coolest place in town. It's off the Strip and small by Vegas standards, but where else can you listen to nonstop classic rock 'n' roll while playing Jimi Hendrix slot machines (a line of "Purple Haze" pays $200) or drinking a cocktail at the swim-up bar?

Luxor (3900 Las Vegas Blvd. S., 702/262-4444 or 877/386-4658): The most distinctive casino, Luxor is housed inside a mammoth (29-million-cubic-foot) glass pyramid at the southern end of the Strip.

The Mirage (3400 Las Vegas Blvd. S., 702/791-7111 or 800/374-9000): This casino has its own rainforest, a 20,000-gallon saltwater aquarium, and white tigers on display (leftovers from the shows of Siegfried and Roy, who last performed in 2003 and retired officially in 2010). Next door, at Treasure Island, a theatrical (and free) pirate show is staged right on the Strip every 90 minutes or so in the evenings.

Wynn Las Vegas (3131 Las Vegas Blvd. S., 702/770-7000 or 888/320-7123): Brought to you by the creator of Mirage and Bellagio, on the site of the historic Desert Inn (where billionaire recluse Howard Hughes used to live), this ultra-fashionable 2,700-suite oasis is the last word in high-end indulgence, with an on-site Ferrari dealership in case you hit a jackpot or two.

One power plant, an experimental, 10-megawatt electricity generating station north of I-40, was built in the 1980s and is now used as an astronomical gamma-ray observatory. If you like shiny cutting-edge technology, you may want to detour from Barstow to Las Vegas along I-15 to see the nearly 400MW **Ivanpah Solar Power Facility,** the world's largest solar thermal plant, which is clearly visible from the freeway.

Barstow

The burly railroad and transportation center of **Barstow** (pop. 22,639) is located in the middle of the Mojave Desert, at the point where I-40 disappears into I-15, midway between Los Angeles and Las Vegas. Trucks and trains are the main business in town—even the McDonald's pays homage to trains, with its dining rooms housed in old passenger cars from a train. Barstow is scruffy and a little scary in the way railroad towns can be. Along Main Street, the old Route 66 corridor, many of the old cafés and motels are now closed and boarded up, but there's an unexplained copy of the Amboy "Roy's" sign, and just north of old Route 66, the circa-1911 **Barstow Harvey House** hotel next to the train station is a survivor from an earlier age. Looking like the Doge's Palace in Venice (if the Doge's Palace faced the wide-open desert instead of an intricate network of canals . . .), the

Outside Barstow at the west end of Main Street, keep an eye out for the Christian Motorcycle club sign welcoming you to **Lenwood,** a crossroads near where the old road reconnects with I-15.

gothic-style arcades are a substantial reminder of a time when travel meant more than just getting somewhere. The long-abandoned building has been brought back to use as a railroad and Route 66 **museum** (760/255-1890, Fri.-Sun. 11am-4pm, free).

Oro Grande: Bottle Tree Ranch

Between Barstow and Victorville, old Route 66 survives as an "old roads" trek across the Mojave Desert. The 36-mile route, called the National Old Trails Highway, parallels the railroad tracks and the usually parched Mojave River, passing through odd little towns like **Oro Grande,** which is still home to a huge cement plant and an array of roadside junk shops. The cement plant, processing local limestone, follows on from the optimistic prospectors who gave the town its "Big Gold" name back in the 1850s. The cemetery here is one of the oldest in southern California. Oro Grande is also home to some long-abandoned roadside businesses, relics of Route 66. One relic lives on: A 1930s tractor dealership now houses the popular **Iron Hog Saloon** (20848 Old Route 66, 760/843-0609), which serves cold beers and big steaks.

The Oro Grande boasts an impressive silver steel bridge over the bed of the Mojave River and is getting famous for another more colorful sight: the hard-to-miss **Bottle Tree Ranch** (24266 Route 66), where thousands of green, blue, brown, and clear glass bottles have been dangled from a forest of mostly metal "trees" by a white-bearded local retiree named Elmer Long. There's no admission charge for the Bottle Tree Ranch, which Elmer has dedicated to "those who have lived and died on the Mother Road." Elmer is not shy (he has his own Facebook page!), so stop and say "hi."

pointing the way to the 66 Motel in Victorville

Victorville

Take the "old road" between Barstow and **Victorville** to be sure to enter Victorville on old Route 66 and see Victorville at its best. At the **California Route 66 Museum** (16825 S. D St., 760/951-0436, Mon. and Thurs.-Sat. 10am-4pm, Sun. 11am-3pm), right on old Route 66, in Old Town across from the train station, a small but growing collection of road signs, photographs, and reminiscences help preserve the life and times of this great old highway. The museum also holds most of the surviving pieces of Hula Ville, an outdoor sculpture park and oddball art gallery that once stood west of Victorville. Most of its paintings and hand-lettered memorials to sundry bums, hobos, and other travelers were moved here after Hula Ville's 100-year-old creator and caretaker, former carnival worker "Fry Pan" Miles Mahan, passed away in 1996.

Without its Route 66 connections, Victorville would be just another distant SoCal commuter suburb. In fact, ever since the departure of Hula Ville, not to mention the wonderful Roy Rogers and Dale Evans Museum, which—along with its much-loved celebrity subjects—had a home here, Victorville just hasn't seemed the same. Fortunately, old Route 66 can still be traced through town: From the Route 66 Museum, turn south onto 7th Street, which runs past a few neon-signed old motels like the **New Corral** (14643 7th St., 760/245-9378, $60) with its animated bucking bronco.

There's also a worthwhile stop two miles east of downtown: Join the truckers and bikers at family-run **Emma Jean's Holland Burger Café** (17143 N. D St., 760/243-9938), rated best in the country by the *Diners, Drive-ins and Dives* TV show.

South and west of Victorville, heading toward Los Angeles and the seemingly distant Pacific Ocean, a number of very picturesque but generally dead-end stretches of old Route 66 go over **Cajon Pass,** but the main road is definitely I-15. At the top of the pass, turn off the freeway at the Oak Hills exit and stop for a burger and fries at the **Summit Inn** (760/949-8688), one of the few survivors of the old road businesses along this stretch of highway.

the first McDonald's, now a museum

San Bernardino

Sometimes known as "San Berdoo," in the 1940s and 1950s the city of **San Bernardino** (pop. 210,000) was where Maurice and Richard McDonald perfected the burger-making restaurant chain that bears their name. In 1961, the McDonald brothers sold their company to Ray Kroc, and the rest is fast-food history. Though the original buildings were demolished decades ago, the location is now home to an unofficial, ad hoc museum, displaying **McDonalds and Route 66 memorabilia** (1398 N. E St., 909/885-6324, daily, free).

From downtown San Bernardino, which somewhat confusingly is actually a dozen miles east of the I-15 freeway, the old Route 66 alignment headed west along Foothill Boulevard, where a remnant of old Route 66 road culture still survives: the 19 concrete tepees that form the **Wigwam Motel** (2728 W. Foothill Blvd., 909/875-3005, around $70). Once as seedy as its "Do It In A TeePee" sign suggested, this Wigwam (one of three in the world—another sits along Route 66 in Holbrook, Arizona) has been fully updated and once again welcomes travelers interested in offbeat accommodations (with free Wi-Fi, a swimming pool, and barbecue grills).

From the Wigwam Motel, Foothill Boulevard runs west through the post-industrial city of **Fontana,** birthplace of the Hell's Angels' Motorcycle Club (and L.A. culture critic Mike Davis), before passing by another great old road landmark: **Bono's Giant Orange** (15395 Foothill Blvd.), an orange-shaped stand that, during the 1920s, offered thirsty Route 66 travelers "All The Orange Juice You Can Drink—10¢." The original orange grove is now a Wal-Mart, and the Giant Orange was moved next to the now-closed Bono's Restaurant and Deli, where it still stands...for now (it's been endangered by ongoing road improvements).

San Bernardino County, which covers over 20,000 square miles (most of it desert), is the largest in the United States

San Bernardino is home to the Class A farm club of the Anaheim Angels. The team name plays up the Route 66 connections: They're called the **Inland Empire 66ers** (280 S. E St., 909/888-9922, $2 and up). The stadium is right off the old road. Games are broadcast on **KCAA 1050 AM.**

San Gabriel Valley

Though it's now effectively swallowed up in Southern California's never-ending sprawl, the **San Gabriel Valley** used to be the westbound traveler's first taste of Southern California. After crossing the Mojave Desert and the high mountains, Route 66 dropped down into what might have seemed like paradise: orange groves as far as the eye could see, a few tidy towns linked by streetcars, and houses draped in climbing roses and bougainvillea. The valley takes its name from old

Rancho Cucamonga (pop. 165,269) is the home of the very popular **Rancho Cucamonga Quakes** (909/481-5000), an L.A. Dodgers farm club that plays Class A baseball at LoanMart Field.

Mission San Gabriel Arcangel (428 S. Mission Dr., 626/457-3035, Mon.-Sat. 9am-4:30pm, Sun. 10am-4pm, $5), which still stands. Despite suffering extensive earthquake damage, the mission is an interesting spot, though not as evocative as others in the chain.

Winding between Pasadena and San Bernardino, along the foothills of the sometimes-snowcapped San Gabriel Mountains, old Route 66 links a number of once-distinct communities like **Azusa,** home of the classic Foothill Drive-In, whose marquee was saved when the land was recently developed, and collegiate **Claremont.** In **Upland,** where the old road features a number of recently installed retro-Route 66 streetlamps, there's a grass median strip graced by a statue of the pioneer Madonna of the Trail, which officially marked the western end of the National Old Trails Highway, the immediate precursor to Route 66.

The city of **Monrovia** (pop. 37,000) holds another Route 66 survivor: the **Aztec Hotel** (311 W. Foothill Blvd., 626/358-3231), known more for its groovy, Mesoamerican-style art deco exuberance than for its rooms, but well worth a look. Monrovia was home for many years to quixotic author Upton Sinclair (1878-1968) and is now the headquarters of the cult-favorite grocery store Trader Joe's. The company, which started in 1958 as Pronto Markets, opened its first Trader Joe's store in Pasadena in 1967.

In the next town to the west, **Sierra Madre,** Foothill Boulevard runs past the landmark racetrack at **Santa Anita,** designed by Hoover Dam stylist Gordon Kaufmann. In 1937 the Marx Brothers filmed *A Day at the Races* here, but the art deco facades have been ruined by

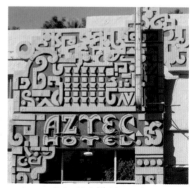
Aztec Hotel in Monrovia

the track's ongoing "development" into a Las Vegas-scale gaming and shopping complex.

Huntington Library, Museum, and Gardens

East of Pasadena, at the west end of the San Gabriel Valley, old Route 66 runs along Huntington Drive, which takes its name from one of the most important figures in early Los Angeles, Henry Huntington. Nephew of Southern Pacific Railroad baron Collis P. Huntington, from whom Henry inherited a huge fortune (as well as a wife, Arabella), Henry Huntington controlled most of Southern California's once-extensive public transit system. He is now most remembered for creating and endowing one of the world's great museums, the **Huntington Library, Art Collections, and Botanical Gardens** (1151 Oxford Rd., 626/405-2100, closed Tues., $20 and up), located in the exclusive community of San Marino.

The Huntington Library contains all sorts of unique books and documents and preserves thousands more for the benefit of scholars, but the real draw is the art gallery, which displays an excellent collection of British and European painting and sculpture, with major works by Reynolds, Gainsborough, and others. There are also fine assemblages of American art, including Gilbert Stuart's familiar portrait of George Washington. Perhaps the best part of the Huntington is its splendid **gardens,** which cover 120 acres in a series of mini-ecosystems, distilling the essence of Australia, Japan, South America, and, in one of the country's largest cactus gardens, the American Southwest.

the Huntington Library's desert garden

Pasadena

Heading out of downtown Los Angeles, the historic Pasadena Freeway (Hwy-110) drops you off unceremoniously short of **Pasadena,** but following Figueroa Street brings you in with a bang on the soaring **Colorado Boulevard Bridge,**

an elegantly arching, circa-1913 concrete bridge at the western edge of Pasadena, which long marked the symbolic entrance to Los Angeles from the east.

Recently restored, the bridge spans **Arroyo Seco** along the south side of the Ventura Freeway (Hwy-134). Arroyo Seco itself is full of significant sights, including college football's Rose Bowl and some of the most important architecture in Southern California, notably the **Gamble House** (4 Westmoreland Pl., 626/793-3334, Thurs.-Sun. afternoons, $14), a 100-year-old arts-and-crafts gem. Above the arroyo, on old Route 66, the **Norton Simon Museum** (411 W. Colorado Blvd., 626/449-6840, closed Tues., $10) has a medium-sized but impeccably chosen collection of western and southeast Asian art, ranging from Hindu sculpture to one of the world's foremost collections of Degas paintings, drawings, and sculptures.

Colorado Boulevard in Pasadena holds the annual **Tournament of Roses Parade,** every New Year's Day before the famous Rose Bowl football game.

Just a few blocks east of Arroyo Seco and the Norton Simon Museum down old Route 66, **Old Pasadena** is the name for the old center of town, where locals congregate for evening fun and daytime shopping. Start your morning with breakfast at **Marston's** (151 E. Walnut St., 626/796-2459), just north of Old Pasadena, or detour two blocks south of old Route 66 to enjoy the fine neon sign and classic soda-fountain milk shakes at the **Fair Oaks Pharmacy and Soda Fountain** (1526 Mission St., 626/799-1414). There are quite a few old motels along this stretch of Route 66; one good bet is the **Saga Motor Hotel** (1633 E. Colorado Blvd., 626/795-0431, $85 and up).

Route 66 Across Los Angeles

Diehard old-road fans will be pleasantly surprised to know that Route 66 across Los Angeles still exists, almost completely intact. West from Pasadena into downtown L.A., you have your choice of

Route 66 routings. You can hop onto the Pasadena Freeway (Hwy-110) for a trip back to freeways past: Opened in 1939, when it was called the Arroyo Seco Parkway, this was California's first freeway and featured such novel (and never repeated) concepts as 15-mph exit ramps and stop signs at the entrances. Or, you can follow Figueroa, which in L.A. lingo is known as a "surface street," running parallel to the freeway past some fascinating pieces of Los Angeles new and old, including the concrete-lined Los Angeles River, hilltop Dodger Stadium, and the excellent **Autry National Center** (323/667-2000, closed Mon., $10) at Griffith Park, a phenomenally wide-ranging collection featuring Native American art and artifacts from all over western North America, as well as Wild West ephemera and pop culture icons. (The center is the result of a merger between the Southwest Museum of the American Indian and the Museum of the American West, established by Hollywood's "Singing Cowboy," Gene Autry, a media magnate who is the only person ever awarded five stars on the Hollywood Walk of Fame.)

Now marked by prominent beige road signs reading "Historic Route 66 1935-1964," old Route 66 follows Sunset Boulevard from the historic core of the city, starting at Olvera Street and the **El Pueblo de Los Angeles State Historic Park** before winding west to **Hollywood.** In Hollywood itself, Route 66 turns onto Santa Monica Boulevard, then runs past the cemetery-cum-theme park **Hollywood Forever** (323/469-1181, daily, free), where such lumi-

naries as Rudolph Valentino and Mel Blanc are entombed, overlooked by the water tower of legendary Paramount Studios. It's a unique experience by day, and even more so on nights when the cemetery is host to outdoor screenings of its residents' works.

Johnny Ramone's final resting place in the Hollywood Forever cemetery

Besides all the sights, Route 66 across L.A. also holds two of the city's best bookshops: **Book Soup** (8818 Sunset Blvd.), in West Hollywood, and **Vroman's** (695 E. Colorado Blvd.), in Pasadena.

Continuing west to the Pacific, old Route 66 follows Santa Monica Boulevard through the heart of **West Hollywood** and **Beverly Hills,** where "Mr. Route 66" himself, the Oklahoma-born comedian Will Rogers, once was honorary mayor.

Los Angeles

Love it or hate it, one thing you can't do about L.A. is ignore it. Thanks to Hollywood in all its many guises (movies, television, the music industry), the city is always in the headlines. Without falling too deeply under the spell of its hyperbole-fueled image-making machinery, it's safe to say that L.A. definitely has something for everyone. In keeping with its car-centered culture, however, our suggested tour ignores the many individual attractions and focuses instead on a pair of quintessential L.A. drives.

the Los Angeles skyline, as seen from Mulholland Drive

Winding along the crest of the Hollywood Hills, **Mulholland Drive** is the classic L.A. cruise. Starting in the east within sight of the Hollywood sign and the Hollywood Bowl, this ribbon of two-lane blacktop passes by the city's most valuable real estate, giving great views on both sides, both by day and after dark.

Another classic L.A. cruise, running from the scruffy fringes of downtown all the way west to the coast, **Sunset Boulevard** gives glimpses into almost every conceivable aspect of Los Angeles life. Starting downtown, the historic core of colonial Los Angeles and now a showcase of contemporary architecture thanks to a stunning new cathedral and concert hall, Sunset Boulevard's 27-mile course then winds west past Echo Park and Hollywood to West Hollywood, where it becomes the Sunset Strip, still the liveliest nightclub district in town. Continuing west, Sunset winds through Beverly Hills, Brentwood, and Bel-Air, lined by the largest mansions you're likely to see, before ending up at the edge of the Pacific Ocean.

The **Los Angeles Dodgers** (866/363-4377) play at beautiful Dodger Stadium, on a hill above downtown.

PRACTICALITIES

Most flights into Los Angeles arrive at Los Angeles International Airport (LAX), on the coast southwest of downtown, where you'll find all the usual shuttles and rental car agencies. Other useful L.A.-area airports include Bob Hope (BUR) in Burbank and John Wayne (SNA) in Orange County.

Before choosing a place to stay, think about where you want to spend your time and settle near there. High-end places abound, but

The Queen Mary

character can be hard to come by. Along the coast, recommended accommodations range from the handy **HI-Santa Monica Hostel** (1436 2nd St., 310/393-9913, starts at $32 per person), a block from the beach, to the unique *Queen Mary* (877/342-0738, $89 and up) in Long Beach, a hotel offering authentic art deco-era staterooms in the fabulous old luxury liner. Midrange with a great mid-city location, try the **Farmer's Daughter Hotel** (115 S. Fairfax Ave., 323/937-3930, $199 and up), next to the historic Farmers Market, a very friendly 1950s-style motel with tons of charm and the city's hottest new shopping mall and entertainment complex, The Grove, across the street. Downtown, the most fabulous place to stay is the retro-1960s **The Standard, Downtown LA** (550 S. Flower St., 213/892-8080, $216 and up), with the world's coolest rooftop, poolside bar.

For food, one place I always try to stop is **The Apple Pan** (10801 W. Pico Blvd., 310/475-3585), an ancient (circa-1947) landmark on the West L.A. landscape, serving the best hamburgers on the planet—though I'll admit to being biased, since I grew up eating them. Take a seat at the counter, and be sure to save room for a slice of the wonderful fruit pies. Late at night, the huge sandwiches and heart-warming soups at **Canter's Deli** (419 N. Fairfax Ave., 323/651-2030, open daily 24 hours) draw all kinds of night owls to a lively New York-style deli in the heart of the predominantly Jewish Fairfax District. Downtown, between Chinatown, historic Olvera Street, and the landmark Union Station, **Philippe The Original** (1001 N. Alameda St., 213/628-3781) serves famous French dip sandwiches in a classic workers' cafeteria, offering good food at impossibly low prices, with character to spare.

The usual array of information about hotels, restaurants, tickets to TV

show tapings, and all other L.A.-area attractions is available through the **Los Angeles Tourism and Convention Board** (6801 Hollywood Blvd., 800/228-2452).

Santa Monica

Old Route 66 had its western terminus at the edge of the Pacific
Ocean in **Santa Monica,** on a palm-lined bluff a few blocks north of
the city's landmark **pier.** The pier holds a small amusement park
and a lovely old Looff carousel (as seen in the movie *The Sting*). A
beachfront walkway heads south of the pier to **Venice Beach,** heart
of bohemian L.A. Near where Santa Monica Boulevard dead-ends
at Ocean Avenue, a brass plaque marks the official end of Route 66,
the "Main Street of America," also remembered as the Will Rogers
Highway, one of many names the old road earned in its half century of existence. The plaque remembers Rogers as a "Humorist,
World Traveler, Good Neighbor"—not bad for an Okie from the
middle of nowhere.

Two blocks east of the ocean, stretch your legs at **Santa Monica
Place** and the adjacent **Third Street Promenade,** an indoor/out-
door shopping area and icon of contemporary Southern California
(sub)urban culture. The surrounding streets are among the liveliest in Southern California; people actually walk, enjoying street
performers, trendy cafés, bookshops, and movie theaters.

Enjoyable in its own right, Santa Monica also makes a very good
base for seeing the rest of the L.A. area. For the full retro-luxury
experience, check in to the art deco **Georgian Hotel** (1415 Ocean
Ave., 800/538-8147, $250 and up). Or you can save your money for
food and fun by staying at the very popular **HI-Santa Monica
Hostel** (1436 2nd St., 310/393-9913, around $38 per person).

carousel at the historic Looff Hippodrome on the Santa Monica Pier

Index

Photo and Illustration Credits

All vintage postcards, photographs and maps in this book from the private collection of Jamie Jensen, unless otherwise credited. Photos © Jamie Jensen: pages 8, 12, 15, 21, 31, 37, 41, 48 (bottom), 50, 52, 54 (bottom), 58 (top), 59, 72 (bottom), 82, 101.

Minor League Baseball Logos

All Minor League Baseball logos are Registered Trademarks of their organizations. Used with permission. Pages 33, 47, 65, 109, 110.

The following images were sourced from www.123rf.com:

10 © Frank Romeo, 24 © Henryk Sadura, 37 (bottom) © Juergen Priewe, 58 (bottom) © Juergen Priewe, 69 © William Silver, 71 (bottom) © Ralf Broskvar, 76 (bottom) © Susan Peterson, 77 © Steven Love, 80 © Mitch Aunger, 86 © Scott Griessel, 104 © Songquan Deng, 114 © Stranger View, 115 © Andrew Kazmierski, 116 © Kay DeBoer.

Public Domain images:

The following images are in the public domain because one of the following applies:
· The work is a work of a U.S. government soldier or employee, taken or made during the course of the person's official duties. As a work of the U.S. federal government, the image is in the public domain.
· The work was published in the United States between 1923 and 1977 and without a copyright notice. Unless its author has been dead for several years, it is copyrighted in jurisdictions that do not apply the rule of the shorter term for US works, such as Canada (50 p.m.a.), Mainland China (50 p.m.a., not Hong Kong or Macao), Germany (70 p.m.a.), Mexico (100 p.m.a.), Switzerland (70 p.m.a.), and other countries with individual treaties.
· The copyright has expired, often because the first publication of the image occurred prior to January 1, 1923.
· The copyright holder of the work has released the work into the public domain. This applies worldwide. In some countries this may not be legally possible; if so: The copyright holder grants anyone the right to use the work for any purpose, without any conditions, unless such conditions are required by law.
· The work is a postage stamp published before 1978.
See http://copyright.cornell.edu/resources/publicdomain.cfm for further explanation.

3 Courtesy Boston Public Library, Prints Division; 17 University of Maryland Digital Collections; 40 (bottom) Courtesy OkiefromOkla/Wikimedia Commons; 49 Courtesy Count Calen/Wikimedia Commons; 57 Courtesy Leaflet/Wikimedia Commons; 66 and 68 Courtesy Boston Public Library, Prints Division; 72 (top) Courtesy Anna Foxlover/Wikimedia Commons, 89 Courtesy Kkaufman11/Wikimedia Commons, 95 © Jittipong Rakritikul.

RoadTripUSA.com

Easily find trip ideas, maps, and route
suggestions, whether you're at home
or on the road.

JOIN OUR TRAVEL COMMUNITY
AND SIGN UP FOR OUR NEWSLETTER

MOON.COM

Road Trip USA
Route 66

Avalon Travel
a member of the Perseus Books Group
1700 Fourth Street
Berkeley, CA 94710, USA
www.roadtripusa.com

Editor: Kevin McLain
Fact Checker: Megan Mulholland
Copy Editor: Naomi Adler Dancis
Graphics and Production Coordinator: Domini Dragoone
Cover Design: Erin Seward-Hiatt
Interior Design: Domini Dragoone
Moon Logo: Tim McGrath
Map Editor: Mike Morgenfeld
Cartographers: Mike Morgenfeld, Stephanie Poulain
Indexer: Greg Jewett

ISBN: 978-1-63121-093-8
ISSN: 1946-3286

Printing History
1st Edition — 2009
3rd Edition — May 2015
5 4 3 2 1

Printed in China by RR Donnelley